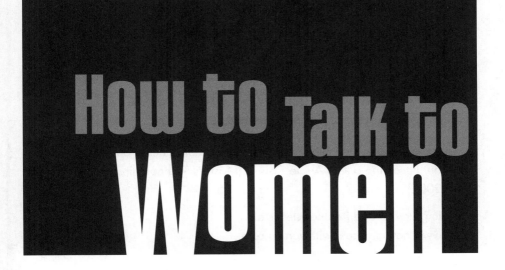

How to Talk to Women

RON LOUIS DAVID COPELAND

MASTERY TECHNOLOGIES PRESS

Other Works By
Ron Louis and David Copeland

How to Succeed with Women (1998, Prentice-Hall Press)

How to Succeed with Men (2000, Prentice-Hall Press)

The Sex Lover's Book of Lists (2001, Prentice-Hall Press)

The Mastery Program: Your Step By Step Course in Meeting, Flirting with, Dating and Seducing the Women of Your Dreams (Mastery Technologies, Inc., 2001)

The Internet Seduction Toolkit (Mastery Technologies, Inc., 2001)

Overcoming the Nice Guy Syndrome: How to Stop Being Shy without Becoming a Jerk Audio Course (Mastery Technologies, Inc., 2002)

Dating advice and free newsletter at
www.howtosucceedwithwomen.com

ACKNOWLEDGEMENTS

Our families, Jim Lemmer, Deborah Lawyer, Theophilus, Paul Schlegel, Pete, Hatcher, Mike Krakalovich, Gene Brissey, Chad Garcia, Kirk Bromley, A. Gile, Dr. K, Scottworld, Cliff Barry, Allen Thompson, Kristyn Kalnes, Chip Rowe, Leslie Ishige, Susan Sherman, Mohammed Ali, Dmitri Bilgere, Roan Kaufman, and Karen Krizanovich.

We'd also like to thank our friends at Playboy, Maxim, Stuff, Cosmopolitan, Playboy, Men's Health, Men's Fitness, and YM magazines. Also to our friends at the Sam Adams Brewery—thanks for the good times!

A SPECIAL "THANK YOU" FROM RON LOUIS AND DAVID COPELAND

We'd like to thank you for reading this book. To listen to a new, not-transcribed-in-this-book real-life example of Louis & Copeland using these flirting skills, go to
http://www.howtosucceedwithwomen.com/talk

For more information write to:

Mastery Technologies, P.O. Box 55094, Madison, WI 53705

Email: authors@howtosucceedwithwomen.com

Web: www.howtosucceedwithwomen.com

Louis, Ron
  How to talk to women / Ron Louis & David Copeland. —
1st ed.
  p. cm.
  ISBN 0-9719076-0-9

  1. Dating (social customs)—United States. 2. Women
—United States—Psychology. 3. man—woman relationships
—United States. 4. Interpersonal communicastion—United
States. I. Copeland, David, 1963- II. Title.

    HQ801.L68 2002   646.7'7
                            QBI33-726

Fourth printing 2005

Printed in Canada

Disclaimer

Remember, you and only you are responsible for your actions and your behaviors. To be crystal clear: The authors and publishers of this book are not responsible in any way for how you choose to use this material. It's always your responsibility to make sure that the actions you take with women are legal and consensual. It is your responsibility.

TABLE OF CONTENTS

	Introduction	1
Chapter 1	Interrupting Women, Risk, Curiosity and Self-Expression	9
Chapter 2	The Hi Program & Vitality	51
Chapter 3	The Inner Game of Talking to Women	71
Chapter 4	Handling Panic and Rejection Around Women	93
Chapter 5	Flirting, "What's the Story Behind That?"	118
Chapter 6	Romantic Moves, Goodbye Introduction	130
Chapter 7	Situational Flirting	150
Chapter 8	Deepening	166
Chapter 9	Advanced Deepening	188
Chapter 10	Romantic Questions, Part 1	220
Chapter 11	Romantic Questions, Part 2	241
Chapter 12	Taking Talking Further	271
Chapter 13	Conclusion	289

How to Talk to Women

InTroDuCtion

Many men are just one skill away from having the kind of interactions with women that they want. Jacob was an example of this. Thirty-four years old, successful in his business, fit and a sharp dresser, he didn't understand why he wasn't more successful with women. He noticed that his friends—some of whom were sloppier, fatter and less financially successful—seemed to be able to get women, but somehow he couldn't. He could talk to women but always ended up "just friends." It was discouraging.

Jacob thought he was miles and miles away from his goal of being successful with women; in fact, he wasn't. He had just about every skill he needed to succeed with women and a lot more, but he didn't know how to talk to women so they felt he was "romantic material." That was the one skill he was missing. Once we taught him the basic Flirting Moves and the skills of talking to women, his level of success with them rose dramatically.

You may have a similar problem. Secretly, like Jacob, you may have wondered if there was something wrong with you. You may have thought that there's something about you that you couldn't see but that women could which drove them away. Or, like Jacob, you may fear that you have some basic flaw that continually sets you up to be "just friends" with women.

The good news is that nothing could be further from the truth. Sure, you've got problems. Everybody does. But as you've probably seen, plenty of men with more problems than you succeed with women. The good news is there's no basic flaw inside of you that keeps you from having the relationship you desire. If you can communicate at all, you can create romantic connections with women. You may simply be one skill away.

When you're one skill away from being a good seducer, you're like a car with one flat tire. A car with one flat tire drives as though it has something seriously wrong with it. It's impossible to control, the ride is rough, and chances are you'll never get where you want to go in it. Driving it, you'd be likely to conclude that it has serious, serious problems.

Once you realize that the problem is a flat tire, though, you see that just because the problem was noticeable didn't necessarily mean that it was fatal. By fixing the flat—a simple 10-minute procedure once you know how to do it—you transform the entire car and can get where you want to go easily.

When Jacob learned that the flat tire in his dating system was his inability to talk to women in a way that made them think romantic thoughts about him, he was able to correct the problem and his interactions with women improved instantly. He had the missing piece and was able to seduce women.

Your problems, too, may not be as big as you thought. A simple set of new skills may make all the difference. If you've ever learned any skill then you can learn how to talk to women; you've simply never been taught how before. It's like learning any new procedure. Once you master the basics, the rest seems easy. This book will teach you what you need to know.

WHAT YOU'LL LEARN FROM THIS BOOK

In Chapter 1, you'll learn about what it takes to initiate interactions with women. You'll learn about the importance of "interrupting" women and being able to redirect their attention toward you. Most men fail at this because they don't know what to do once they have a woman's attention; don't worry, we'll cover that, too. You'll also learn about opportunities and the surprising truth that not taking opportunities with women can naturally lead to taking them, if you do it our way. You'll learn about curiosity and how you can tap into your natural curiosity with a woman to easily create stress-free conversations in which you both experience a real connection with each other.

In Chapter 2, you'll learn about the Hi Program, which is the perfect place to start building your skills in talking to women. You'll also learn ways to increase your sense of vitality and excitement with women, including simple ways to make the sound of your voice something that women enjoy hearing.

However, only knowing what to say to women is not enough. You must also understand the "inner game" of talking to women, or you won't be able to get yourself to take action with them. In Chapter 3, you'll learn how to overcome your tendencies toward being defensive with women and apologizing for your interest in them, as well as ways of communicating with women that don't require worrying or strategizing. In Chapter 4, you'll enhance your grasp of the inner game of talking to women by learning once and for all how to overcome the fear of being rejected by women. You'll also learn how to handle panic around women so you can use the skills in this book, even if you get nervous.

In Chapter 5, you'll learn how to leverage the hidden seductive power of the simple question "What's the story behind that?" You'll also learn the three time-frames of an interaction with a woman so you'll always know how much you need to risk with a woman at any given moment.

In Chapter 6, you'll learn about the Romantic Moves that are a critical part of talking seductively with women. You'll learn about looking into a woman's eyes "too long," checking out her body so she feels complimented, winking at her and more. You'll learn how a man who does these Romantic Moves almost never ends up "just friends" with a woman, and you'll learn why a woman tends to put a man who makes these moves into the potential lover category in her mind. You'll also learn the Goodbye Introduction, which is a simple, powerful, romantic and incredibly low-risk way to introduce yourself to beautiful women.

In Chapter 7, you'll learn the specifics of Situational Flirting. You may have noticed that men who are successful with women are often good at joking around with women. They are able to kid with women about different aspects of the situations that they find themselves in or about objects in the immediate environment. This is Situational Flirting. In Chapter 7, you'll learn the specific steps of joking around with women and ways of creating romantic, flirtatious running jokes. You'll see specific examples of Situational Flirting and learn how to do it yourself with the women you encounter.

In Chapters 8 and 9, you'll learn how to use the incredibly powerful romantic conversation tool called Deepening. Deepening is a conversational mode that allows you to get into a woman's world and find out what she's passionate about. Deepening allows a woman to open up to you right away in a way she may not open up to many people in her life. You'll learn how to use Deepening to admire a woman's passions, which many other people may never see, thus creating a deep connection between you. You'll read numerous actual transcripts of us having Deepening Conversations with real women alongside our comments on these examples, so you can learn how to apply this skill in your own life.

In Chapters 10 and 11, you'll learn about asking Romantic Questions and conducting Romantic Conversations. You'll learn how to ask Romantic Questions in ways that don't seem corny or intrusive but that move the conversation in a romantic direction. You'll read numerous actual transcripts of us asking Romantic Questions and conducting Romantic Conversations. Our comments on these examples will help you learn to practice these skills when you flirt and go on dates.

In Chapter 12, you'll learn about taking talking further: moving from a flirting conversation to getting a woman's phone number and email address to setting up a date. You'll also learn important secrets about going for the first kiss.

By the time you're through with this book, you will have an entire toolbox for talking to women in romantic, flirtatious and fun ways. These skills are specific and they are learnable. With practice, you will be able to use them successfully.

HOW TO USE THIS BOOK

There are two types of communicators. You must figure out which type of communicator you are, because each type must practice and use the skills in this book differently.

THE INTROVERTED COMMUNICATOR

Most of our students, and most of the men who are attracted to our work, are introverted communicators. These are men who categorize themselves as shy. They have a hard time talking with women and are more likely to end up a wallflower than the life of the party. These men often have no clue about what to say to women and need to start very slowly, taking one small step at a time and building from there.

The primary challenge for the introverted communicator is learning to express himself. He needs to intensify and escalate his signals by 500 percent. He needs to focus on talking more loudly, making more eye contact, overcoming his shyness, being curious, asking questions, showing romantic interest and taking risks. In short, he doesn't need to worry about toning himself down; he needs to worry about turning himself up.

THE EXTROVERTED COMMUNICATOR

The extroverted communicator tends to be enthusiastic, silly and fun. These are often men who are in sales, teaching or other fields that involve lots of interactions with people.

Extroverted communicators adore being the center of attention. They aren't necessarily scared to talk to women, but they often don't know what to say. They often think that the way to seduce a woman is to turn up the volume of their personality. This is what the introverted communicator needs to do—but for the extroverted communicator, it's a real mistake.

If you're an extroverted communicator, try listening more, talking more softy and chilling out. Don't try so hard. In short, the extroverted communicator doesn't need to worry about turning himself up; he needs to worry about toning himself down.

As you read this book, keep in mind which type of communicator you are. This will influence your decisions about how aggressively you use this material.

our work

We are also the authors of the book *How to Succeed with Women*. That book provides a step-by-step approach to finding, meeting, dating and seducing women and has been very successful. The one thing that was missing from *How to Succeed with Women*, however, was detailed information on how to talk to women. We had a few paragraphs on the topic, but that was not enough.

This book rectifies that problem and exhaustively explores the topic of talking to women. What it does not do is repeat the information from *How to Succeed with Women*. If you want to learn about where to meet women, setting up successful Priming Dates and Seduction Dates, handling the problems and trouble women cause, getting the first kiss, proceeding to sex with women and a lot more, we suggest you get that book.

We are also the creators of a step-by-step 32-day audio course, *The Mastery Program*, which you might be interested in. This course, available on 16 CDs or 16 cassettes, takes you day by day through a program designed to install the dating fundamentals in your life and help you talk to and be successful with women. For more information on The Mastery Program, check out our web site, www.howtosucceedwith-women.com, or write us at the addresses below.

You also may be interested in our 4-cassette or 4-CD course, *Overcoming the 'Nice Guy' Syndrome: How to Stop being Shy without Becoming a Jerk*. In this program you will learn skills and participate in exercises that will help you overcome being shy, and allow you to feel good about showing your romantic interest to women.

And, of course, you might be interested in the *How to Talk to Women* CD. To make this compact disc, we brought women into the studio and flirted with them, creating Romantic Conversations using the techniques you will learn in this book. We then went over these conversations and added our commentary and "play by play" so you can hear us flirting with women, and also learn what we are thinking and how we are deciding our next steps as we do it! These Romantic Conversations are all new. While the techniques we use are taught in this book, the conversations on the CD are not transcribed in it. Check out www.howto-succeedwithwomen.com/talk to find out more about this useful product!

We also do one-on-one dating coaching with a select group of highly motivated men. If you are interested, email us at Authors@howtosucceedwithwomen.com.

You can find out about any of our products and services, sign up for our free email newsletter and learn more about seduction by visiting our web site at www.howtosucceedwithwomen.com. You can email us at Authors@howtosucceedwithwomen.com. Our U.S. mail address is Mastery Technologies, P.O. Box 55094, Madison, WI 53705.

And now, please enjoy *How to Talk to Women*.

How to Talk to Women

CHapter 1
Interrupting Women, RISK, Curiosity and Self-Expression

If you are like most of our students, talking to women seems complicated, confusing and difficult. Yes, there will be challenges as you learn to talk to women, but if you're willing to start at the beginning and do the work involved, over time you'll succeed. Unfortunately, many of us think that the best way to go about learning is to skip the first step, or even the first few steps, and to go directly to "the good stuff." Building a firm foundation in the first few simple steps of talking to women will help dramatically once you start applying those steps to the more complex skills we will present later in this book.

A bad seducer—let's call him Bob—has trouble because he hasn't mastered the basics. If you are like Bob, you want to avoid saying hi to women, and you only want to ask the one fool-proof (and mythical) seduction question that will make any woman strip and have sex with you in 30 seconds or less. If you are like Bob, you expect to overcome 25 years of shyness and failure with women after reading five pages of this book.

We wish we could teach you that one question that would get any woman to fall in love with you and have sex with you in 30 seconds or less. We wish we could help you overcome fear and shyness after reading five pages of this book—but we can't. We can, however, teach you a series of progressive steps you can use to learn to talk to women. We can teach you questions, approaches and conversational modes that will help you be seductive—but you must be willing to start at the beginning. Once again: If you want to become good at talking to women—that is, if you want to learn how to talk to women seductively—you have to start at the beginning.

Seducing women by talking to them is a process. The first step of that process is answering the question "How do you get that initial contact with a woman?" After we have answered that question, we will go on to learn ways of talking with her, ways of flirting with her and ways of constructing and conducting romantic, seductive conversations. Get ready—this plane's about to take off.

"Just Be Yourself"

We hate trite, useless advice like "Just be yourself" or "Just go talk to her!" This kind of advice is worse than useless because it offers nothing specific to do yet leaves you feeling bad about yourself for not following it. Sure, being yourself is a good thing, but how should you do that with women? More specifically, which part of yourself should you be? We all wear many hats in our lives. When you approach a woman, should you be the self you are at work? The self you are at church? The self you are at a strip club? We all need to cultivate the romantic parts of ourselves— the parts that are naturally fun and seductive, but just saying you should do so is not enough. If just being yourself had worked, you wouldn't be reading this book. "Just be yourself" is pretty worthless advice.

The same goes for "Just go talk to her." We've all been given this lame advice, but most of us have no clue what to talk to a woman about. The other day, a shockingly beautiful young woman we know was wondering aloud to us why our books, audio courses and other material are necessary at all. "All you have to do is go up to people and talk and just be yourself," she told us. "It always works for me!" As she said this, her full breasts rose and fell with each breath and her beautiful blonde hair swayed as she moved her head.

We also know a man who is a model in a large city. When we go out with him, we're always amazed—hot women approach him and give him their phone numbers. He also likes to tell us his "secret": "Just be yourself and talk to women! It's really not a big deal!"

Obviously, both these people make most of us want to vomit with rage. You don't have to work hard at learning how to talk to the opposite sex if you are in the top .01 percent of beautiful people; if you're that hot, the world will beat a path to your door. For the rest of us, there are specific skills to learn, which are much more effective than "Just be yourself" and "Just go talk to her."

Our work has always been about breaking complex social interactions into teachable steps so those who employ our methods can succeed. Our students have discovered a new level of ease and freedom with women when they've learned to use this material. We'll start small, so that no matter how shy you have been, no matter how shut down you've been, no matter how many problems you've had with women, you will be able to take action and move forward.

We remember how hard it was to talk to women and how much courage it took for us to transform our skills and our abilities. We remember how we wished we had help in figuring out what to do, and we remember how we had to start with very small steps before we could move on to longer conversations. We had to figure out talking to women through trial and error. At first we constantly failed. We were each as uncomfortable and awkward when talking to women as any guy we've ever met. We failed more often than you've failed, and we made fools out of ourselves time after time—but we stuck with it and transformed our dating lives. We mention this not to toot our own horns but to give you hope. No matter where you are in your life, no matter how little experience you have with women, there is hope. You can learn to seduce women. You can learn how to talk to women. And you can have the success you want.

Self-Expression

You can't be an effective seducer unless you feel self-expressed around women. A man who is self-expressed has character. By that we mean that he's an individual who follows his own path. He feels confident making decisions about where he wants to take his life. He embraces the ways in which he is similar to as well as the ways in which he is different from others. He is able to be himself without being overly concerned about how women will respond—and he's not trying to control or fix women. He is authentic and honest. He doesn't squelch himself, suppress himself or hide from life.

When we say that you should be self-expressed, this also means that you must find your own way with the material in this book. None of our books or audio courses are designed to be a set of rules to box you in. We all have different approaches with this material—even we, Ron Louis and David Copeland, have very different approaches from one another. We agree on the fundamentals but we approach them differently.

The main commonality among all effective seducers is that each embraces his unique approach and style. The best way for you to communicate with women is to find your unique style. Otherwise you'll seem fake and feel awkward when talking to women.

Let's digress for a second and look at the opposite of self-expression: withholding, feeling bottled up and unable to talk to women. We've found that men are most upset, frustrated and plain ol' nuts when they aren't self-expressed. Not getting laid doesn't drive guys nuts; a guy can go months without getting laid. What drives men nuts is not interacting with women, not talking to women, hiding out at home and not being in the game. What drives men nuts is having the desire to make contact with women and not doing anything about it.

Avoiding the risks of life drives men crazy—not failing or being rejected. When you're engaged in life, taking risks and interacting with women, women will find you attractive. What fails every time, however, is staying on the sidelines of life feeling bottled up and depressed.

Interrupting Women

Your first task on the path to becoming a seducer is to understand and accept that you, the man, are going to have to interrupt women in order to get their attention and start a conversation.

Let's examine the word "interruption." It's a harsh word. Most of us associate interrupting people with being rude, obnoxious or disrespectful. For many of us, this is especially true regarding interrupting women. When we say interruption, we don't mean to imply being rude or obnoxious at all. We use the word interruption, though, because it communicates a harsh truth about talking to women: when you first interact with a woman, you will probably have to do something specific to direct her attention away from whatever else is going on in her life and toward you. You are going to have to take some action—though as you will see it doesn't have to be a big action—to get her attention. There's forcefulness about the word interruption that describes the energy you will need to do this.

As you have no doubt noticed, women are usually not thinking about you. They are off in their own world, on their own vector, in their own flow. Hot women are not likely to come up to you and say, "Hey, you look like an interesting guy. I would love to have a conversation with you and then seduce you." Therefore, if you are going to interact with women, your first task is to get their attention. And you get their attention by interrupting them.

In a certain sense, you are interrupting women on a deeper and deeper level with every stage of a seduction. You interrupt her when you first say hi to her. You interrupt her on increasingly deeper levels when you talk for the first time, when you ask for her number and email address, when you have Romantic Conversations, when you ask her for and conduct the first date, when you go for the first kiss and so on. You are always interrupting her and initiating something deeper. The burden of initiating and interrupting women will be on your shoulders until you die. The tools in this book will help you carry that load. In fact, they can turn this burden into a boon for you—not just with women but with every area of your life.

WHY CAN'T WOMEN INTERRUPT YOU?

Sometimes a man will ask us, "Why should I risk rejection? Isn't this the age of equality? Why don't women initiate with me, and interrupt me?"

You know, it's funny—women talk a lot about how men don't feel enough. They complain that men aren't more sensitive and bemoan how all that "male privilege" and "male power" have made men shut down emotionally. Well, you know the truth as well as we do. Men's egos aren't a mess because men are so all-powerful or because men live lives of complete and total privilege and ease. Men's egos are a mess because they don't have any tools for handling rejection, and they have to throw their ego in the sewer every time they approach—and risk being rejected by—a woman. So of course men aren't going to be emotionally sensitive. Constant rejection makes you want to be a little less emotionally sensitive, right? What an astonishing surprise.

Here's the bottom line: women don't approach you because dating is not fair. That's why. They don't want to throw their egos in the sewer, and they don't have to because they're women. They are allowed to demand equality as much as they want and still leave all the risking of initiation to you (at least in the early parts of dating).

We suggest that you accept that this is the way it is and that instead of being upset about it, you realize that this actually gives you a certain kind of power. If you have to do all the interrupting and initiating, you get to say when you will approach a woman. You get to say when you will ask her out; you get to say when you will flirt with her. Once you start seeing that having to do all the initiating and having to take all the risks gives you the power to go after what you want, the fact that women don't have to initiate with men will not bother you so much.

Okay, our little men's rights speech is over. We agree that you have every right to be mad about this state of affairs—but staying mad doesn't work. It won't get you the girl. The good news is that when you know how to take the proper risks with women, one step at a time, you don't have to shut down your emotions and become an unfeeling jerk in order to initiate with women. And once you know how to do it, you'll be able to go after the women you want with a lot more freedom than most women feel they have to go after the men they desire.

Your ability to initiate with and interrupt women is critical. Everything in this book is built on that skill. Successful seducers understand the stages of seduction and are willing to start at the beginning. Before we give you specific ways to start interrupting women, it will be helpful for you to learn a little about a few core concepts: the numbers game, opportunities not taken, and giving and receiving risks.

THE NUMBERS GAME

As you learn to interrupt and initiate with women, you must remember that all your interactions with women basically boil down to a numbers game. A certain amount of the time you will succeed; the rest of the time you won't. The great thing is that if you have enough interactions, your success is all but assured.

It's like the insurance salesman who knows that he needs to make 75 cold calls to get one appointment and that it takes four appointments to get one sale. Therefore, he knows that he needs to make 300 cold calls, give or take, to get one sale. He knows it's a numbers game and that all he has to do is to continue making those calls. Eventually the numbers will work in his favor and he'll make a sale. With women, it might take 10 interruptions to get one conversation, 10 conversations to get one phone number and 10 numbers to get one date. This is good to know because each "failed" interaction brings you closer to success.

In *How to Succeed with Women,* we wrote time and again that dating is a numbers game. We're saying it again now. It's empowering to know that dating is a numbers game because knowing that will help keep you going toward your eventual success. Every time an interruption or initiation with a woman doesn't work, remind yourself that that "failed" interruption brings you one step closer to the inevitable success.

The key difference between successful seducers and unsuccessful ones is that the successful ones know it's a numbers game and keep going no matter what. Unsuccessful seducers whine to their friends, hide in their bedrooms or feel upset and give up approaching women entirely. Train yourself to see that approaching women is a numbers game.

Opportunities not Taken

Men often feel bad about themselves when they see an opportunity to approach or talk to a woman and they don't take it. They don't take the opportunity because they are scared or upset or because they simply don't know what to say. This leads to missed opportunities and plenty of good old-fashioned self-criticism. "I was such an idiot not to talk to her," these guys will say to themselves. "What a moron I am. I can't believe how stupid I was not to talk to her. It was a perfect opportunity. She was so hot. I'll probably never get an opportunity like that again, and I blew it!"

There are lots of times in life when beating up on yourself to get yourself to behave better is a good idea. There are lots of times when it works. Unfortunately, this is not one of those times. When you don't take an opportunity with a woman and then punish yourself for not taking it, you just attach a lot of pain to the whole idea of taking opportunities to talk to women. This makes you less likely to talk to a woman the next time an opportunity comes up, not more.

There's a sequence in the way most men treat opportunities with women. First, you don't see opportunities at all. It seems like there are no women on this planet for you to interact with. Second, you start to see opportunities but don't yet have the ability to take them. If you allow yourself to let that be okay, in time you simply find yourself starting to take those opportunities that life presents to you. However, if you beat yourself up for not taking opportunities, this sequence is disrupted. Beating yourself up for not taking opportunities just makes it harder to see and take them in the future.

People who train group facilitators know that this is true. At first, students may have no idea at all about how to lead a certain type of process in a group; they simply watch in awe as other people lead. In time, they start to understand how to lead but they don't quite know the process well enough to step out and actually lead; they watch from the sidelines, full of good ideas about how they would lead a process but not quite ready to take charge themselves. If they allow this to happen without beating up on themselves, in time they simply notice that they are stepping out and leading—and nothing special needs to happen for that to occur. If they beat themselves up, however, they stall the entire learning process and make it harder to take action when the time comes.

Once you break the link between seeing an opportunity and feeling bad about not taking it, you can break the hold that this cycle has over you. We suggest that you let yourself go through a phase of purposely not taking opportunities with women. Just observe them and let yourself feel good about yourself even when you aren't taking them. Say to yourself, "I'm able to see opportunities, and that's an important step. I'll take opportunities later." In time, your nervous system will be so used to spotting opportunities that it will be much easier to take them.

Seeing opportunities to interrupt women is a little like slowing down reality. We had a student who was an expert in the field of stock trading.

He was able to see and take advantage of financial opportunities that just seemed to flash by too quickly for us to see or understand what was happening. He had a completely different relationship with markets than we did. To us, the stock markets are just one big mess; we can't see opportunities in them. Because of his years of experience watching the market, this guy was able to slow things down. He told us that he did this by not beating himself up when he missed opportunities. This is what you must do too.

GIVING AND RECEIVING RISKS

In this book we are going to teach you effective tools that can help you have deep, romantic and seductive conversations with women. But to wield these tools effectively you must understand the nature of risking with women.

Doing any of the things we talk about in this book will require taking some risk. Most men are extremely averse to risking with women; they live their lives trying to avoid it. Many men who aren't successful with women are committed to eliminating risk with women; that's their unsuccessful strategy for success.

Men are obsessed with not risking with women mainly for two reasons. First, they don't want to be hurt by a risk gone wrong. It totally sucks to take some big risk with a woman only to be shot down in one of the almost infinite number of ways women have of shooting down men. Second, men—especially shy men—want to eliminate risk with women because they are afraid that they will somehow hurt the woman they risk with. They are afraid that if they take a risk, the woman will be upset, offended or emotionally damaged in some way.

For these men, the apparent answer to both of these problems is decreasing risk and increasing control over their interactions with women. They start looking for the foolproof, always-completely-in-control, no-risk system for seducing women. Like a bad salesman who seeks that "magic close" that will force a customer to buy, buy, buy, a guy who can't risk with women will look for psychological tools that can force a woman to be attracted to him. He'll buy pig-pheromone colognes, hoping the scent will awaken a woman's inner vixen. He'll play "subliminal seduction" audiotapes for her, hoping it will somehow create chemistry between them. Or he'll try to learn hypnosis, hoping to use it to bamboozle a woman into taking her pants off. He does all this in an attempt to eliminate all risk with a woman and to establish in its place complete control over all of his interactions with her.

There are several problems with this. First, eliminating all risk with a woman and establishing complete control over your interactions with her doesn't work. In fact, it's the opposite of what works with women. Think about how you feel when you're with someone who's committed to completely controlling your interaction with him and the outcome of that interaction: you can't get away fast enough. Well, that's exactly how women feel with a man who's committed to eliminating risk, controlling the interaction and forcing a certain outcome. (Salesmen are sometimes like this.) It doesn't matter how good a pre-scripted rap you come up with; it's spooky for a woman to be with a guy who is trying to control her.

Second, most men get discouraged with methods of seducing women in which the mantra seems to be "control, control, control." Men want to be able to express themselves and create successful, seductive interactions with women. As one man told us, "If I wanted to hide behind a 'fake self,' then I might as well go to a prostitute." If you want anything deep or spontaneous with women, eliminating all risk and controlling everything is not the way to get it.

At the same time, it also doesn't work to "just do it"—to take huge risks with women all of the time. We used to know a guy whose life's philosophy was "Go for the roar." This meant that every time he saw something scary or risky, he had to do it—because if he didn't, as he put it, he "wasn't really living his life." We think this is ridiculous, and the trouble it created in his life backs us up on that. Just because you can take a huge risk with a woman doesn't mean that you should.

Just as risking because you can isn't the answer, letting go of all control in your interactions with women is probably a bad idea too. Letting go of guiding or directing conversation in any way will all too often get you another female "friend," and we've all had quite enough of that.

If eliminating risk entirely and controlling everything doesn't work with women, and taking all the risks you can and letting go of all control doesn't work, what does? The answer is that you must take risks, but you must take them in a sensible, appropriate and orderly fashion. Surprisingly and paradoxically, you actually provide more of a sense of both safety and excitement to women when you take intelligent and appropriate risks with them one step at a time. That's what creates both chemistry and trust.

Taking and Giving Risks

Many men think that when they take a risk with a woman they are somehow taking something from her, but the truth is this: when you take an appropriate risk with a woman you are giving something to her. Your risk with her creates a space for her to take a risk back with you, which builds trust, safety and attraction with you. If you don't take a risk with her there's no space for her to risk with you, and she can't have a relationship with you, even if she wants one.

Think of it this way: often a guy will wait around for a woman to risk with him before he risks with her. He wants her to say hi, he wants her to ask him out, he wants her to go for the first kiss. But why should a woman do something you aren't willing to do? Remember, most of the time a woman is looking to you to set the pace and feel for your interaction. If you take a small risk with her, she will see an opening to do the same with you. If you take no risks at all, try to keep control of everything and work to force a certain outcome with her, she will do the same with you—and it won't be the outcome you want. She will be controlling and defensive, and her goal will be to get away from you.

As a general rule, women will only risk as much as you do, if that much. When you take an appropriate risk with a woman, it actually provides an opening for her to be self-expressed and have fun with you. This is what we mean when we say that you must provide risks for women. When you take an appropriate risk with a woman, you give her the opportunity to risk back with you. That's providing a risk, and it's the foundation for creating chemistry and trust with women.

When the two of you take a small risk together—for instance, you may provide a risk by winking at her and she may risk smiling back—a little trust is built between you. You can then build on that trust to provide a slightly larger risk. For instance, you may provide a risk by asking her "What's the story behind that?" about her necklace, and she may take a risk by telling you about how she got it on a trip to Central America. When that risk has gone well, there is even more trust between you. You can then provide the next larger risk and she can risk back. In time, a sense of trust and safety develops.

Simultaneously, this process creates a real sense of excitement and chemistry between you. The two of you are constantly in the process of being "on the edge" with each other, constantly revealing a little more of yourselves with every risk, always trusting and risking a little more each time. That process is where excitement and chemistry come from. That process is where a lot of attraction comes from. And that is a process you can learn how to manage without being controlling, trying to eliminate risk or attempting to force an outcome.

ALL-OR-NOTHING MEN

Building a relationship with a woman is a lot like building a house in which your intimacy and connection can live. You build that house one brick at a time. Every time you take a risk and she takes one back and it works, you put another brick in the walls of the house. After a while you've built four walls of trust that can contain the relationship you have with her.

If you risk too much too fast, you are trying to live in the house before it is built, and trouble will come if any problems occur. At the same time, if you don't risk at all, you never even build a foundation for a relationship, much less the four walls and roof. The level of risk you should take is related to how much of this house you have built. If you have a lot of trust built up from taking many risks together you can proceed to some bigger risks. If you don't have a lot of trust built up you need to take smaller risks.

It's important to underscore that trust is built over time and that chemistry and attraction are not the same as trust. A man who doesn't have much facility or experience with risk will trust a woman way too fast. He'll trust her utterly and completely with his entire heart the moment he experiences any chemistry with her. That's a really bad idea.

We had one student who was dating a women whom he was certain was "the one" after only one date. He was having tremendous success with her as he measured it: she seemed to like him, it was very exciting and delightful to be with her and they were having amazing sex together. He jumped in deep, really opening his heart to her in a matter of days, totally risking himself emotionally. After all, what could possibly go wrong in such a whirlwind romance?

Well, plenty could go wrong and plenty did go wrong. After a couple of weeks, this "perfect woman" disappeared. She rarely returned his calls and started blowing off their dates. Finally she told him, "I like you, but with my life the way it is, it's just too much of a hassle to have a relationship right now. Besides, I'm sort of seeing this other guy..." He was devastated, heartbroken and even more afraid of taking risks with women than he had been before.

When you meet a hot woman with whom you have great chemistry, your tendency might be to take big emotional risks with her as quickly as you can. That is a big mistake. It's insane to risk your entire heart right away. Take small risks one at a time and build trust over time. If you risk too much too quickly you'll have your heart splattered all over the pavement, and you'll have short, passionate affairs that end with you being heart-broken and alone.

That happens when you jump in too deep too fast, and you do that when you mistake chemistry for trustworthiness. Just because you have chemistry with a woman doesn't mean she won't flake out on you. It doesn't mean she won't have emotional problems that will cause her to leave. It doesn't mean you can count on her. But when you have great chemistry with a woman, you're all too likely to think that it means you can count on her, and you'll end up risking too much with her.

The solution is to go slowly and build trust with a woman before you give her your heart fully. In other words, you must risk slowly, over time, in the way we will show you. If you are going to fall in love with a woman you are really attracted to, you need to take risks one step at a time to find out if you can trust her. You need to know if she's a psycho who's going to go nuts and take off on you, breaking your heart. You can only find this out by risking the proper amount at the proper tempo.

On the up side, most women are incredibly attracted to a man who can say, "I really like you, and I want us to take the time to learn to really trust each other so we can truly open up and be intimate. I want to take things slowly and build a connection we can trust." Saying this sort of thing tends to make a woman feel really safe with you and desire you all the more. After all, you aren't just trying to get as much sex out of her as you can, like all those other guys. She likes this; therefore, she wants to have sex with you. A man slowing things down and risking with her one step at a time can be an incredible aphrodisiac to a woman.

Slowing down a romantic relationship with a woman you are attracted to might suck, but it doesn't suck as much as 1) having a short affair that ends in heartbreak or 2) being so afraid of heartbreak that you develop a massive fear of taking any risks with women.

THE ECONOMY OF RISKS

Let's look at how to provide risks for women. Most nice guys do not take enough risks and they do not provide enough risks for women, so women have too few opportunities to take risks back. How do you provide risks to a woman? You provide risks by taking risks. That's important, so let's say it again: You provide risks by taking risks.

It helps to think of risk as a currency that you exchange with a woman. You put up a penny and she puts up a penny. You put up a dollar, she puts up a dollar. You put up ten dollars, she puts up ten dollars. You're exchanging these quantities. The exchange can get bigger as you learn from each other that it will be a fair exchange, an exchange you can trust. If you put up your penny and she takes it and runs, you know not to put up a hundred dollars. But if she puts up a penny back, you know you can take the risk to put up a nickel. If she gives you a nickel back, you can then put up a dime.

Let's give some specific examples now of the kinds of risks you can take at different levels: penny risks, dollar risks and $10 dollar risks. ("Great," we hear you saying—"now talking with women is like banking and investing." Who would've known?)

Bizarrely, though, that is what talking to women is like. Successful investors learn to take intelligent financial risks; most of the time they learn how to do that by taking small risks and moving up to larger ones as they get better at it. As a result, they get better returns than do people who never invest their money, who never take any risks with it and who leave it in the bank earning interest at three percent or less. By learning about intelligent risk, successful investors are able to leverage their assets, taking the risks that deliver the best returns.

Penny Risks. You can think of the first risks you take with a woman— the interruptions that allow you to speak with her—as penny risks. Saying hi is a penny risk. So is making eye contact, winking at her, smiling at her, checking out her body and the other Flirting Moves. Each one of these small actions takes a risk with a woman and gives her the opportunity to risk back with you by being responsive in some way. If she does respond with a risk of her own, you are in business and can move on to the dollar risks.

Dollar Risks. The dollar risks are larger, but if the penny risks went well, why not move on? Complimenting a woman is a dollar risk, as is asking a question we'll teach you, "What's the story behind that?" The Goodbye Introduction, which you'll learn, is a dollar risk, as is Situational Flirting, Deepening and asking Romantic Questions. These risks all provide her with the opportunity to risk more by sharing more about herself with you. So she starts to risk liking you, which means she could get hurt. These risks are what generate the excitement in a relationship.

$10 Dollar Risks. Asking for her number and email address, setting up a date, showing up for the date, doing something together on the date, touching her, going for the first kiss and being even more sexual are all bigger risks. These risks and all the risks that lead up to her sharing her life with you, even if only for a little while. She starts to risk that you might change her life in ways she did not plan on.

This is an exciting process for both of you. And with each new risk you evaluate how it went before taking the next one. If a small risk did not pan out, don't go on to take a bigger risk. Instead, you might want to take a smaller risk and see if that works. This is all a matter of risking step by step.

It's important for you to realize the risks you provide when dealing with women. Each risk offers a space for magic to happen between the two of you, and it's a gift that you as a man provide. You're not perpetrating evil or hurting someone else; you're providing that excitement that women need so much.

Intelligent Risks Lead to Rewards

Everything we will teach you in this book is to some degree a risk you will have to take with women. By knowing that and by being able to take those risks one step at a time, you will have the power to create excitement and trust in your interactions with women. Of course, some of those risks won't work out, but we'll teach you how to handle rejection too. It's all part of learning how to talk to women.

As you use the tools in this book, your mantra should not be "control, control, control." That will only get you into trouble. Your mantra should be "risk, risk, risk." Intelligent risks, taken step by step. By using these tools to risk being romantic rather than to control the interaction, you will be able to manage the orderly unfolding of a relationship. It may be short-term, it may be long term. It may be deeply intimate, it may be purely sexual. But there will be a real connection—and you won't have to sell yourself out to get it.

Curiosity

An important aspect of self-expression is curiosity. It's similar to enthusiasm: you've got to use it or lose it. Once you've repressed your curiosity long enough, it takes time to get it back.

Many of us were taught as children not to ask questions, to avoid being too curious. We all know the expression "curiosity killed the cat." Asking questions and being curious were often said to cause trouble.

Another "problem" with curiosity is that when you start asking questions you stop being in control of the interaction. When you ask a woman questions about herself, suddenly you're not in control of what she might say. As we've said, most guys come to us wanting a line or routine. They're looking for a structure they can impose on an interaction that will keep them in control and get her romantically interested. But when you take the risk of not knowing what is going to happen, and surrender to the chaos of interactions and conversations with women, you're more likely to connect with them and more likely to come across as fun and attractive.

You can start the process of letting out your curiosity by asking women questions and simultaneously letting go of any outcome. Let go of trying to get into her pants and getting her number (for a second) and just see if it feels different. We're not saying that trying to get into her pants is a bad thing at all—we're just saying that when you concentrate on getting into her pants as your sole outcome it's very difficult to maintain a conversation and therefore hard to get into her pants.

You never know where a conversation is going to go with a woman, but if you've got to stay in control and restrain your own curiosity and never ask a question you don't already know the answer to you'll never be successful. Most men just give up because not knowing where an interaction is going is just too scary.

Another advantage of learning to be curious is that it's not the least bit manipulative or scam-oriented. When you take risks with women and they risk with you, real intimacy can develop.

If being curious is difficult for you right now, don't worry. After you start experimenting with being curious it will become a lot easier.

How to Ask Women Questions

We're now going to explore how to ask women questions. This is not rocket science. So many men feel like they need to know the right things to say to a woman. The truth is that you don't need specialized esoteric questions; you just need to know how to be curious and ask questions.

Let's look at the different kinds of questions you can ask. There are initial questions, the first questions you ask someone. Then there are follow-up questions, which follow up on the response to your first question. Pretty simple so far, right? You got it. The basic sequence is you ask a question, she responds and you ask another question. It's almost like having a real live conversation where you are opening your mouth and talking! One question leads to another and before you know it women are revealing themselves to you. They are risking themselves to you and you are risking with them by asking questions and revealing yourself.

Here are some handy, easy-to-use rules for asking questions and having good conversations with women.

Asking Questions is not the Same as Offering a Compliment

It's great to compliment women, but most of our students find it intimidating to compliment a woman right away. Luckily, you don't have to start a conversation with a compliment. Instead, you can ask questions. Of course, you shouldn't insult women either. If you ask a woman "How did you get your hair so ugly?" or "How did you get so stupid?," you aren't going to go anywhere good. We include these only for comic relief. When you first meet a woman it usually makes sense to start with a simple question.

Asking Questions Is Not the Same as Making Statements

Many of our students make the error of making statements rather than asking questions. For example, a student recently told us that he'd asked a woman a question the other day. Here's how he described it: "We were at a concert and I said to her, 'The floor sure is sticky.'" Well, that's not a question, and that doesn't offer much of an opening for her to respond. You need to ask questions that evoke a response from her, not simply make statements.

Asking Questions Is Different From Talking About Yourself

If you were at a concert and you walked up to a woman and said, "I sure like the band," Louis and Copeland would come to your house and break your finger. This is a statement about yourself, not a question about her. You must learn the difference. This point seems simple, but many guys mess it up. You need to ask her something that will engage her in a back-and-forth conversation, not spew your opinions about life.

At first, a woman won't be interested in you or your opinions. Instead, she'll be interested in talking about herself. This means that your focus should be asking questions that let her do just that. Rather than talking about your favorite color, ask her what her favorite color is. Rather than raving about the great new CD you just brought, ask her what sort of music she likes. Rather than talking about your favorite season, ask her what her favorite season is.

DO NOT ASK STUPID, CHEESY QUESTIONS

When you're interacting with a woman and asking questions you are not allowed to ask "Do you come here often?" You are also prohibited from asking about the weather. Those two questions are so clichéd that you will come across as a total bonehead. The last thing you are forbidden from asking is "What's your sign?" These all sound too much like lines and come across as boring and stupid. The good news is that there are countless good, simple questions. Once you get your curiosity circuitry going, you won't have a problem asking them.

DO NOT ASK OVERTLY SEXUAL QUESTIONS

You might find yourself wondering, "Gee, are those breast implants? How do they stand up so well?" That's obviously not a question you're going to want to ask. We probably don't have to tell you this, but we wanted to double- and quadruple-check.

We're not suggesting that you avoid thinking about sex or avoid wondering about a woman's breasts or what she's like in bed. Those are things we all wonder about when we talk to women. Don't even try to suppress those thoughts. We're just saying that none of those questions will fly. Just remember that you risk face slaps, explosive forms of violence, sexless nights and trouble if you make overtly sexual comments.

Asking Questions Is Not an Interrogation

It helps to say something like "Wow" or "Really" or "That's interesting" before asking a follow-up question. When you use those phrases, take a breath between questions and listen to her response, so a woman won't feel as if you're grilling her. Put away the interrogation-room spotlight and make sure you avoid bombarding her with rapid-fire questions. Some men will keep asking a woman "Why? Why? Why?" or barrage her with questions until she flips out. That's another way to have her feel like she's locked in an interrogation room with you. If you ask one question at a time and go at a slow, relaxed pace, the conversation will feel natural and easy to sustain.

When some guys are excited they feel pumped up. While being energized is a good thing, sometimes guys in this state tend to ask too many questions too quickly and not allow women enough time to respond. Just remember to slow down, give her time to respond, add a few appreciative comments and you'll be fine.

Avoid Yes-or-No Questions

"Do you like art?" "What sorts of art do you like?" Can you tell the difference between those two questions?

Let's try this on Ron and David.

DAVID: So Ron, do you like art?

RON: Yes.

That clearly doesn't build much of a conversation. Let's try it again.

DAVID: Ron, what kind of art do you like?

RON: I'm a big Jackson Pollock fan. I like his huge abstract paintings.

DAVID: What else do you like about his work?

RON: I love seeing the movies of him splashing huge cans of paint onto canvases. I'm also interested in how he lived his life.

DAVID: So have you seen his work in person?

RON: Yes, I've been to several exhibits of his work in New York.

So you see where this can go. A yes-or-no question just doesn't cut it. For instance, "Do you like the band?" is a problem. A way to take that question out of the yes-or-no realm is to ask "What do you like about the band?" or "How to do you like the band?" Start paying attention to the questions you ask women. Make sure you avoid putting them in a form that will have them answer yes or no.

women are not always friendly

This may come as a shock to you, but our experience shows that many women are not the slightest bit receptive to anything we say. It's important therefore to remember that when a woman is mean to you or unresponsive, it's not a personal attack on you. We all have to deal with unfriendly women at one point or another.

Remember, it's not your fault she was unfriendly, and you did nothing wrong by approaching her. When a woman is unfriendly, the best thing to do is to move on to the next one. It's pointless to waste your time and energy talking to women who are unreceptive. In fact, it can damage your self-esteem to hang around women who treat you like crap. Next time a woman is mean to you, remind yourself that there are other women out there who'd be happy to talk to you and would appreciate your initiating with them—and then move on.

The purpose of asking questions is to generate a conversation

Don't worry if a woman strays from the question you've asked her. Some students get upset when they muster the courage to ask a woman a question and then, rather than answering their question, the woman responds by talking about a wholly different topic. Remember, when you ask a woman a question and she responds with any comment at all, it's good news. Your focus should be on getting a conversation going.

For example, imagine you're asking to a woman in the liquor store about wine and she starts talking about a movie she just saw. Don't say, "Hey, I asked you about wine—just answer the question, lady!" The point is that you want to be engaging with her, and it really doesn't matter what you talk about. The fact that you are actually having an interaction with her is good news. Having her open her mouth and talk to you is as good as it will get at first.

nurturing your curiosity

For us, curiosity often shows up as a small flicker in our minds that we must pay close attention to. If you don't pay attention when you feel curious about something, your interest fades. At this stage of the game you're retraining yourself and creating new habits to let your curiosity out. At first, accessing your curiosity might feel awkward and clumsy, but it will get easier over time.

Asking a question of a woman and listening to your curiosity doesn't need to be a big deal. It doesn't require you to find complicated or unusual topics to explore. In the following examples you'll see how we've taken incredibly mundane situations and created simple questions to ask women. After reading through these examples and doing some experimentation on your own, this will be a lot easier for you.

Example 1

SITUATION: You're at a concert, listening to the music and standing next to an attractive woman. What do you do? Here's the sequence we recommend you start employing when talking to women:

First, breathe deep into your body. Many men breath shallowly, and high in their chests—this really doesn't leave you feeling powerful—for that, you need to breathe more deeply. We call this "breathing into your balls." When we say this, we mean take a deep breath, and imagine that feeling going all the way down to the core of your body, all the way down into your balls. It may sound silly, but it's been our observation that it makes a big difference.

Second, ask yourself what you could be curious about with this woman.

Third, listen to the response you get.

Here's a chain of curiosity questions that you could use at the concert:

"So, what do you think of the band?" When she answers, "They're great," run through the sequence again:

- Breathe into your balls.
- Ask yourself what you could be curious about in her response.
- Listen to the answer.
- Ask your follow-up question.

For example: "What are other bands you've seen that you like?" This question then generates another response from her. You might ask, "Have you seen this band before?" She might answer, "No, I haven't seen them before." So you then repeat the sequence:

- Breathe into your balls.
- Ask yourself what you could be curious about in her response.
- Listen to the answer.
- Ask your follow-up question.

For example, "What do you think of them?" or "The bass player's got really wild hair. What do you think about it?"

See how simple this can be? Once you realize that you don't have to put yourself on the line and show off, talking to women becomes a lot easier. What's important is for you to ask questions that make her impressed with herself—and when you focus on asking questions that make her impressed with herself, your life will be much easier.

Example 2

SITUATION: You're in line waiting to buy something in a grocery store and you're standing next to a woman. You want to talk to her. What do you do?

- Breathe into your balls.
- Ask yourself what you could be curious about with this woman.
- Listen to the answer.
- Ask your initial question.

For example, you might say, "That's an interesting pin that you're wearing. What's the story behind it?"

She might say, "Oh, I got this in Nepal."

So you go through the sequence again:

- Breathe into your balls.
- Ask yourself what you could be curious about in response to what she said.
- Take a second and listen to the answer.
- Ask your follow-up question.

You might say, "Nepal, how interesting. Do you like to travel?" or "Nepal, that's really an interesting place. What were you doing there?"

From there you may find yourself creating a conversation with her!

Example 3

SITUATION: You're in line waiting to buy something and you're standing next to a woman with a new cell phone hanging on a clip from her purse. So what do you do? Go through the sequence:

- Breathe into your balls.
- Ask yourself what you could be curious about with this woman.
- Listen to the answer.
- Ask your initial question.

"I see you have one of those new cell phones, how do you like it?" She responds, "It's great, it gets much better signal than the other one I had."

Repeat the sequence:

- Breathe into your balls.
- Ask yourself what you could be curious about in her response.
- Take a second and listen to the answer.
- Ask your follow-up question.

You might say, "What happened to your old phone? Did it break? Or did you find there were parts of town where it didn't work?"

These are not very personal questions, but you can see how these can lead to deeper conversations. You can also see how simple and natural they are.

Example 4

SITUATION: You are in a bookstore next to a woman reading a book. Go through the sequence:

- Breathe into your balls.
- Ask yourself what you could be curious about with this woman.
- Take a second and listen to the answer.
- Ask your initial question.

You might say, "That book looks really interesting. What do you think of it so far?" She might respond, "Well, it's pretty good."

Run through the sequence again:

- Breathe into your balls.
- Ask yourself what you could be curious about in her response.
- Take a second and listen to the answer.
- Ask your follow-up question.

You might respond, "So, what do you like about the book?" or "Is that author good? Have you read other books by that author?" or "What have you been reading lately?" or "Is there anything you can recommend to me?" Those are the kinds of questions that start a conversation.

Example 5

SITUATION: You are in a coffee shop and you are ordering coffee from the hot woman behind the counter.

Start by running through the sequence:

- Breathe into your balls.
- Ask yourself what you could be curious about with this woman.
- Take a second and listen to the answer.
- Ask your initial question.

For example, "You must see all sorts of stuff working here. What's the most unusual thing you've seen while working here?"

She might respond with something like "A guy came in here once and ordered 10 cups of coffee and drank them all within eight minutes." So what do you say next?

You go through the sequence again:

- Breathe into your balls.
- Ask yourself what you could be curious about in her response.
- Take a second and listen to the answer.
- Ask your follow-up question.

You might say something like "What would have happened if you had drank that much coffee?" or "If that was your weirdest day working here, what was the best day working here?" or "What's the coolest thing you've seen while working here?"

Or you might have asked, "Do you drink a lot of coffee while working here? I bet there's a lot of temptation."

She might have answered, "I can't drink coffee anymore, and I used to love it."

Run through the sequence:

- Breathe into your balls.
- Ask yourself what you could be curious about in her response.
- Take a second and listen to the answer.
- Ask your follow-up question.

You might say, "What do you drink now instead?" or "Why did you stop drinking it?"

One thing to notice here is that once again these are simple questions. Also, notice that when you ask them you're not sharing a lot about yourself. You don't need to try to be impressive yourself. She doesn't care that you drank 25 cups of coffee one day and how cool you are for being a speed freak. She's interested in herself. Remember to focus on drawing her out with your questions, not on showing off.

Example 6

SITUATION: You're at the gym. After you finish a workout, a woman walks up and prepares to use the same machine you were on. So what do you do? Run through the sequence:

- Breathe into your balls.
- Ask yourself what you could be curious about with this woman.
- Take a second and listen to the answer.
- Ask your initial question.

Perhaps you say something simple like "What's your favorite machine here?" She responds, "I love doing bicep curls. That's my favorite."

So you go through the sequence again:

- Breathe into your balls.
- Ask yourself what you could be curious about in her response.
- Take a second and listen to the answer.
- Ask your follow-up question.

You might ask, "What is it about the bicep curl that you like?"

A simple question like that could start a conversation. The more we practice having simple, easy interactions with women, the more powerful we see that they can be. Just simple curiosity—not trying to impress anyone—can lead to getting a woman's phone number, a date, a connection, rapport and more.

Example 7

SITUATION: You are waiting to be seated at a café. A woman is standing next to you who looks like the type of woman you'd like to be talking to. You notice that there is a lot of unusual art on the wall. So you run through the sequence:

- Breathe into your balls.
- Ask yourself what you could be curious about with this woman.
- Take a second and listen to the answer.
- Ask your initial question.

You might say, "Hi, what do you think about all this art?" She might respond, "It's not my style, but I guess it's okay."

Then you go through the process again:

- Breathe into your balls.
- Ask yourself what you could be curious about in her response.
- Take a second and listen to the answer.
- Ask your follow-up question.

You might respond, "What kind of art do you like?" or "What kind of art do you think might look better up there?"

Example 8

SITUATION: You are at a restaurant and an attractive waitress is waiting on you. You see her and want to talk to her. So you start by running through the process:

- Breathe into your balls.
- Ask yourself what you could be curious about with this woman.
- Take a second and listen to the answer.
- Ask your initial question.

You say something like "What's your favorite food, even if it's not on the menu?" She responds, "I love a really good steak."

Run through the process again:

- Breathe into your balls.
- Ask yourself what you could be curious about in her response.
- Take a second and listen to the answer.
- Ask your follow-up question.

You might respond, "So what is the best steak you ever had?" or "What's the best restaurant you've ever been to?" or "What's your favorite restaurant in town?" or "What's your favorite place in town for steak?"

Example 9

SITUATION: You're at a liquor store looking for tequila. An attractive woman working there asks if she can help you. You run through the process:

- Breathe into your balls.
- Ask yourself what you could be curious about with this woman.
- Take a second and listen to the answer.
- Ask your initial question.

You might say, "I'm looking for some good tequila. What kind do you like?" She might respond by telling you the brand she likes. You can then run through the process again:

- Breathe into your balls.
- Ask yourself what you could be curious about in her response.
- Take a second and listen to the answer.
- Ask your follow-up question.

So you might come up with the question "What do you like about it?," which would be a perfect next question. You could also ask, "Which place serves the best tequila or margaritas in town?" This could build into a deeper conversation.

Example 10

SITUATION: You're at the video store looking for a DVD or a video. You see a cute woman stocking videos. You decide to talk to her. Here's what you do:

- Breathe into your balls.
- Ask yourself what you could be curious about with this woman.
- Take a second and listen to the answer.
- Ask your initial question.

You might ask her, "What is your favorite new release?" or "What's the best movie you've seen recently?" She'll probably answer the question and mention a newly released movie, so you run through the process again:

- Breathe into your balls.
- Ask yourself what you could be curious about in her response.
- Take a second and listen to the answer.
- Ask your follow-up question.

You respond, "What did you like about that movie?" or "Is that the kind of movie you normally like?" or "What kind of movies do you tend to rent?" This will get her telling you about herself. Then you can ask her more questions. Over time, these sorts of conversations can get much more intimate and personal.

CONCLUSION

We strongly recommend you practice being curious with both men and women. A game that we like to play (though we don't tell other people we are playing it!) is seeing how long we can go in a conversation without revealing anything about ourselves. In the game, you're only allowed to ask questions of another person.

We were recently listening to a speech given by marketing guru Jay Abrams. He was talking about the power of questions and the power of listening. Abrams told a story about a time he was traveling cross-country and met a guy on an airplane. Abrams starting asking the guy questions about himself. They talked for hours—nearly the whole trip. At the end of the conversation, the man turned to Abrams and said, "You are the most interesting guy I've ever met." Abrams commented that the ironic part was that he (Abrams) did not say anything about himself; he just kept asking questions.

We mention this story to show how people will bond with you and feel comfortable with you when you give them the gift of asking questions. When you provide women an opportunity to talk and express themselves, they will not only feel bonded to you but they will also feel appreciative that someone listened to them. They may not consciously realize that you only listened to them and only asked questions without sharing much about yourself. Still, as in Abrams's story, they will be conscious of feeling closer to you.

We ask a lot of women if they've ever been on a date with a guy who just talked about himself, never shutting up or asking her anything. They all say yes. They mention that it's rare for a man to be a good listener. As part of your curiosity skills, take the time to listen to how women answer your questions.

Good news: you are now free of having to generate magical conversation to impress a woman. Better news: you are now free to ask questions, listen to the responses and ask more questions. •

CHapter 2
THE HI Program & vitality

You've learned about the importance of interrupting and initiating inter-actions with women. Here's a simple way to start putting that knowledge into action, starting today.

Let's talk specifically about how you interrupt women and redirect their attention toward you. Many men think that what they really need is a great opening line. Guys often ask us, "What are the opening lines that women like?"

Here are some opening lines we know women don't like, just for your amusement:

- "Hey baby, let's do breakfast tomorrow—shall I call you or nudge you?"
- "Hi, my name is David. Remember it, because you'll be screaming it later tonight!"
- "Hey baby, are you wearing your space underwear tonight? Because your ass is out of this world!"
- "Hey sexy, how would you like to join me in doing some math? Let's add you and me, subtract our clothes, divide your legs and then multiply!"
- "If I could rewrite the alphabet, I would put U and I together."

- "There must be something wrong with my eyes. I can't take them off of you."
- "Excuse me, do you have a quarter that I can borrow? I told my mother that I would call her when I found the girl of my dreams."
- "Congratulations! You've been voted most beautiful girl in this room. The grand prize is a night with me!"
- "Hey baby, is your dad a baker? Cause you sure have great buns!"

We are getting nauseated.

Let's be absolutely crystal clear: we are not suggesting you use these lines. We include them to draw your attention to the basic problem with opening lines: no matter how cute, sexy or obnoxious your opening line is, after you've used it, you are still face to face with a woman. When you use some opening line, she either laughs, snorts or throws a drink in your face. Then you still have to come up with something to say next. If anything, cutesy opening lines make it harder to connect with a woman, because so often they are stupid lines that piss women off.

The University of Chicago did a study of opening lines (your tax dollars at work!) and found that "Hi" is the most effective opening line with a woman. "Hi" is followed in effectiveness by "Do you like the band?" (But only if there's a band playing—try to keep that in mind.)

The bottom line is there is no opening line that can keep you from having to generate a conversation with a woman, so you might as well use hi—at least it won't piss her off. Of course, you'll still have the problem of needing to generate a conversation with her, but we'll get to that. First, let's talk about that best of all opening lines, the word "hi."

The Hi Program

Getting into the habit of saying hi to women is an important first step in having longer conversations with women, conversations that lead to seduction and sex. Therefore, learning to say hi is your first task in interrupting and initiating with women.

This is obvious but important to note: saying hi to a woman establishes a precedent of communication that can work to your advantage. After you say hi to a woman, it's natural to continue talking with her—but it'd be weird to talk if you hadn't said hi. Therefore, saying hi is your first step toward seduction and sex.

For instance, have you ever been in a situation where, if you'd only said hi to a woman right away, it would have been appropriate to talk to her later on? Perhaps it happened while you were waiting in line. You got in line and you noticed a very pretty girl in front of you, but you didn't say hi to her when you first saw her as you got into the line. You were in your own world or you were too afraid to say hi or you didn't want to interrupt her or you used whatever your standard excuse is for not interrupting and initiating with women. You stood in line next to this beautiful woman for a little while and you realized that you wanted to talk to her—perhaps you even thought of something the two of you could converse about—but by then you couldn't, because it would have seemed weird to start talking to her after ignoring her for so long. If only you had said hi when you first got into line you would have had some precedent of acknowledging each other's existence, and it would have been much easier to talk more later.

You've probably had that kind of thing happen. We have, too. Such sad, lost opportunities are the result of not setting a precedent of being a guy who talks to women. They're the result of not saying hi.

If you are going to learn to talk to women and implement what you learn and become good at it, you have to be able to take scary actions and boil them down into steps that are so small that they are not scary any more or are just scary enough that you can still do them. The Hi Program is a great way to do that.

The Hi Program is really simple: you decide how many woman you are going to say hi to each day and you do it. Suppose you decide to say hi to 10 women a day. Later on, while you're walking down the street, you see 10 women and you say hi to them. You go to the mall, you see 10 women, you say hi to them.

When you follow the Hi Program, you become the kind of guy who just naturally finds himself saying hi to women, so when you're in that line you have already said hi to that cute girl in front of you and you can easily move on to some other conversational sequence.

THE FIVE RULES OF THE HI Program

1. Decide how many women you are going to say hi to each day and keep track of how you do. Many of our students say they will say hi to 10 or 20 women a day for five or six days a week. Decide how many women you will say hi to for how many days a week and write it on a piece of paper or an index card. Carry that card with you and keep track of how many women you actually say hi to as you go through your day.

This may seem silly, but it's important. If you don't have an idea of how many women you said hi to, it's very easy to get stopped and stay stopped. If you keep track, you can look at your index card and say, "Wow, I said I would say hi to 10 women a day and I said hi to zero women yesterday and two today." Then you can look through this section again, figure out what your problem is and correct it. If you don't keep track, it'll be easier to delude yourself, overlook trends and blow the power of the entire program.

On the other hand, keeping track also helps you feel good about what you've accomplished. Especially if you've been a shy guy, looking at your card and seeing you said hi to 37 women today can feel pretty good. It's worth doing.

2. The women you say hi to don't have to hear you say hi. At this point, the important thing is that you open your mouth and say hi. What's not important at this juncture is whether women hear you. So open your mouth and say hi whether you think she can hear you or not. The women you say hi to can be walking in the other direction or even wearing headphones. It doesn't matter. Just say hi.

A lot of guys say, "Well, all the women I saw this week—all of them, 100 percent—were wearing headphones and were Rollerblading the other way or for some other reason wouldn't have heard me, so I didn't say hi." Well, that's garbage. These guys didn't say hi because they were scared, and they used a woman's inability to hear them as an excuse for not following the program. Open your mouth and say hi. It doesn't matter if she hears you or not.

3. Say hi to any woman you see. That's right, any woman. She can be old, fat, disabled—it doesn't matter. Remember, this is about building your initiation muscle so you can interrupt women and redirect their attention, no matter how briefly, toward you. At this point, it can be with any woman at all; it doesn't matter.

4. Celebrate that you did it. Often we talk with a guy who would only let himself feel good about himself if he managed to convince a totally unattainable, uninterested supermodel whom he met on the street to sleep with him in 15 minutes or less. Then and only then would he allow himself to feel good about what he accomplished with women.

We've said it before and we'll say it again: that kind of attitude is a mistake. If you are learning to talk to and seduce women, you must allow yourself to feel good and to celebrate each step in the process of getting laid. Beating yourself up and feeling bad will not help because a guy who is really down on himself is inherently unattractive to women. So reward yourself; praise yourself for saying hi. It will help start you on your way to becoming a master at talking to women.

If you try to practice the Hi Program but put down your effort and success just because you aren't getting laid yet, you will only impede your own process. Let yourself feel good about taking action. Tell yourself things like "Wow, I said hi to 10 women! I am the man!" Find something to celebrate about the progress you are making in interrupting and initiating with women. You might want to keep a journal about it, perhaps writing, "I am the man because I said hi to 25 women today. I can see that I really am breaking out of my shell, and that's great." Or you can get your body involved: make some little motion, like shaking your fist powerfully while saying, "Yes! I said hi!"

We're amazed by the extent to which the men we work with resist feeling good about the small steps and small actions they take with women, but it's important that you do so. Most men have a hard time celebrating any accomplishment that isn't an ordeal. That won't work with women. Women like to be around men who feel good about themselves, so it makes sense to reward yourself and feel good about taking this first step in talking to women: saying hi to them.

You must do this. So many of our students will say things like "Well, I was walking down the street and I said hi to 20 women in five minutes and it was easy, so therefore it doesn't count." Or they say, "Yeah, I said hi to 10 women, but they were all old or ugly, so it doesn't count." They discredit their work before they even see the positive effects of it.

Many men who have a hard time talking to women are often caught in this trap: it's either got to be too hard, and thus they can't do it, or it's too easy, so it doesn't count. It's as if they haven't suffered enough to allow themselves to feel good about what they did. Don't make this mistake.

5. Practice out loud. Some men are stopped by the idea of saying hi to women they don't know. They start to say hi and they choke up.

Actually, such chokes happen to everyone now and then. You open your mouth to say hi and nothing comes out. It's embarrassing, but there it is.

If you have trouble saying hi to women, practice saying hi out loud alone in the comfort and privacy of your own home or car. Just say hi over and over in a clear, powerful voice. This will get your body used to saying hi and make it easy and natural to do. Soon you'll be able to do it without thinking about it, which is what you need when you get face to face with a beautiful woman. You'll be able to say hi to women on the street, in bookstores, at classes or anywhere else you meet them.

How you can screw up the Hi Program

Our experience has shown us that men are very inventive in screwing up the Hi Program. Here are the most popular traps guys fall into. Learn these and avoid them and you will be fine.

1. Disqualifying all women. You can screw up the Hi Program by disqualifying every woman as a candidate for a hi. Usually it works like this: a guy refuses to say hi to most women because they are not hot enough. He then refuses to say hi to the rest because they are so hot that he's intimidated. The solution is to remember this: your job is to say hi to something female and human. That's all.

2. Waiting for the "perfect moment." The truth is there's never a perfect moment to say hi. You just have to do it. If you can't just say hi, you're going to have a really hard time generating conversations with women. Waiting around for the perfect moment to say hi guarantees that you'll never say hi because the perfect moment never comes. You have to make that moment happen by interrupting her flow and creating it.

Most contact with women is not going to happen unless you make it happen. You need your interruption muscle to be strong so you can create that contact. This is critical. Remember, you alone are responsible for interrupting women and initiating contact with them. You have to do it.

3. Only saying hi to women who make eye contact with you. This is a very common problem men have with the Hi Program. Guys say to us, "You guys told me to say hi to 10 women a day and I thought that would be really easy, but then no woman made eye contact with me, so I couldn't say hi to any of them."

Listen: if you are going through life waiting for women to make eye contact with you before you say hi, you are waiting for women to initiate with you before you will interact with them. You are trying to avoid interrupting women, and how well has that been working in your life? Not very well. The terrible truth: you must say hi to women even if they aren't looking at you. Women are rarely going to make eye contact with you before you say hi. They are going to avoid contact because that is what women are programmed to do. Say hi anyway.

4. Being upset by women's responses. You'll get all sorts of responses when you say hi. Some will be warm, some not. One of the benefits of the Hi Program is you start to learn that her response doesn't matter. What matters is that you took action—you took a risk in saying hi.

DAVID: The other day I was leaving my gym and I saw a very pretty girl standing in the gym's foyer looking at a poster on the wall. As I went by her I said, "Hi!"

She started in shock and turned toward me, horrified. She looked completely terrified, which is strange, as I happen to know that I am not that scary-looking a guy. But this is part of being the kind of guy who says hi, who goes for what he wants without shame or apology. Some women are really in their own world of fear and upset. It has nothing to do with you, and there's absolutely nothing you can do about it. If I hadn't startled her, something else would have. So I did what you have to do in those situations: I reminded myself that dating is a numbers game, that this kind of response happens occasionally and that it was about her, not me. Then I went on with my day and didn't think about it any more.

RON: Here's another example of the weird kind of response you might get when you say hi. The other day, I was walking in a nearby woods and I said hi to a woman who was also walking there. Her response? She turned and ran away from me—and I am not that scary-looking either. It was this beautiful nature area; I smiled and said hi and she just looked incredibly upset.

We are here to tell you that it's time to stop worrying about women's responses, even if they are like the ones detailed above. It's time to get past this idea that you are going to shatter a woman's entire personality just by saying hi. Some women, because of their own problems, their own history and their own lives, will get a little spooked when you say hi. It doesn't matter. If you hadn't spooked her, something else would have. That's her, not you.

It's worth risking this kind of response because hi can also work for you. We have had many more experiences where just saying hi has initiated wonderful, seductive conversations with women. You just need to remember that everybody who practices the Hi Program occasionally gets a weird response, and so will you.

5. Refusing to take any risks. Men also kill the Hi Program by being unwilling to take risks. Many men worry about what other people will think and aren't willing to risk that people might think poorly of them because they say hi to women.

For instance, you may feel like you are risking that everyone will see what you are doing, everyone will know you are trying to be a seducer and everyone will point at you and laugh or throw rocks at you or whatever. However, if you are going to initiate with women and get them into bed, you're going to have to take these risks—and more like them.

For now, simply know this: interrupting women feels risky because it is risky. By following our advice, you'll learn how to take small risks with women and gradually move into bigger risks over time. The small risk of saying hi is the perfect place to start.

6. Deciding the Hi Program is so simple that you don't need to do it. A lot of our students say, "Well, saying hi to women is really easy so it can't really be effective. I mean, I could do that right now." We always respond, "Okay, great. If it's so easy, say hi to 10 women a day for the next week." Inevitably they come back the next week and tell us, "Wow, it was a lot scarier and more challenging than I thought, and more valuable, too."

THE RESULTS OF THE HI PROGRAM

The results of the Hi Program can be amazing. One of our students, a guy who had not had sex in a couple of years at least, was a great example of this. We gave him the assignment of saying hi to 10 women a day and sent him on his way.

When we talked to him the next week, we asked, "How'd it go? Did you say hi to 10 women a day?" He said, "No, I didn't say hi to 10 women a day. I said hi to more than 300 women in the last seven days. I went to the beach and I said hi to every woman I saw. I went to the mall and I said hi to every woman I saw. Wherever I went, I said hi to every woman I saw. I said hi to 50, 60, even a hundred women a day. I said hi to hot women, ugly women, old women, young women—all of them." He had done great work, and he felt really good about it.

Taking such massive action had positive results. He got his interruption and initiation muscle so strong that he was empowered to boldly and powerfully take the next steps in talking to women as we taught them to him. He became able to take opportunities as they presented themselves and gave himself a bias for action with women that over time got him sex with a number of women and eventually a girlfriend.

Obviously, saying hi by itself wasn't enough, but the point is this: he never would have succeeded without learning to say it. He got himself to the point where he could initiate easily, and that made it possible for him to meet, converse with and seduce women. Strengthening your interruption and initiation muscle is the critical first step in being able to talk to women successfully, and the best way to get that muscle stronger is by saying hi.

If you don't feel like you have the guts to do more, just start by saying hi to a few women a day or even one a day. That will start to develop your initiation muscle, and that will start you on your way to powerfully and reliably talking to women.

Vitality

Men who have had bad experiences with women usually develop habits that make it harder to connect with women. For instance, they never develop the habit of expressing their vitality and their physical energy. In fact, they are often unable to project any form of excitement or "up vibe" about anything. These men have repressed the parts of themselves that display vitality when interacting with others.

We're going to discuss two types of vitality: physical vitality and vocal excitement. We'll show you how to have more physical vitality and vocal excitement in your life. Both will help you become more powerful with women.

Physical Excitement

If you don't have physical excitement and physical energy, if you don't project a physical presence, it's hard for women to get excited about you. If you are calm and have a flat affect, you've got a problem. Women are looking for someone who has vitality, passion and energy. Put another way, do you come across as a guy who gets laid or as a guy who is painfully shy and hard to talk to?

One way to have more vitality is to act with more urgency around women. Many men treat life like a rehearsal. There's no energy or commitment behind what they do. They act like they can wait around forever before taking action. As a result, they appear to be wishy-washy and they have a flat affect. These men also tend to come across as boring and predictable. If you fall into this category, don't worry. We'll teach you methods of bringing more vitality to your life. It's a skill that you can master if you work on developing it over time.

Five Ways to Bring Physical Excitement Into Your Life

Look over your life and situations in which you were interacting with women. Did you have a sense of urgency when talking with them or were you flat and wishy-washy? Our hope is that this book will inspire you to start taking more risks with women and feel more confident to take on life at a much higher level that you've ever felt comfortable doing before. Here are five things that will help you do just that.

Use Your Body for Emphasis. When you use your hands and body as you speak, you'll come across as more passionate and powerful. Don't go too far, though, by pretending to have an epileptic fit; we're talking about adding hand and body movements for emphasis only. You shouldn't wave your arms around looking insane.

To get a better idea how to use your body to emphasize what you're talking about, watch late-night-TV talk-show hosts and comedians. TV performers are good speakers because they're subtle and graceful and use their body in a very natural way. These people are skilled at adding body movements to emphasize the humor in their monologues. Studying these performers should give you an idea how to integrate your body into your own speaking style.

Make Eye Contact. Part of developing a physical presence is training yourself to make eye contact with women. When you enter a room, do you sweep the room making brief eye contact with women or do you look at the floor and try to hide? Most shy men avoid eye contact no matter what. One of the components of having a physical presence is making eye contact with women as well as men. It's important that you learn to be seen by people and feel comfortable being looked at. When you approach a woman, it's crucial that you feel comfortable looking at her and making eye contact when you speak. Otherwise, you'll come across as wishy-washy and uninterested.

You might find making eye contact scary. If so, you're not alone. Many men find eye contact intimidating. We recommend that you practice this skill as often as you can—on the train, walking down the street, anywhere there are women. Over time you'll feel more comfortable.

Dance and Jump Around. Another thing you can start doing right away is to put on a danceable song and spend at least five minutes each day dancing and jumping around to the music. Many men who are intimidated by women don't give themselves permission to get excited about anything or to feel physically excited about anything. They tend to stay calm and flat. Train yourself to be more spontaneous by dancing to a song every day.

Let Yourself Scream. It's important to let go and make some noise occasionally. You might want to go into your car and scream loudly. It's important that you learn to express yourself and amp up or calm down depending on the situation. One way to learn to be more excited is by amplifying your voice.

Work Out. Working out on a regular basis is another way to charge up your body. When you feel great after a workout or run, you in turn project vitality to the women you interact with and the other people in your life. Working out is important, not only because it helps with stress relief and keeps you in good shape but also because it increases your physical presence when you're with women. Find a form of aerobic exercise you enjoy and do it often.

These five suggestions will help you develop physical presence and power with women. All of these exercises will help you be more self-expressed and will help you come across as more attractive to women. Remember, have fun while you do them and stop when it stops being fun.

Vocal Excitement

When you're vocally excited, you speak with a variety of vocal tones; you don't just talk in a monotone and say the same thing over and over. If there aren't many speed changes or volume changes in your speaking style, you come across as dead. When you approach a woman and are boring and flat, she'll likely want to avoid talking to you. The reason most guys talk quietly is because they're scared of interrupting or upsetting women. One way to feel more confident is to learn to speak from your balls.

Speaking From Your Balls

We first talked about speaking from your balls in chapter 1. It sounds strange, but it's very effective. We've all had moments when we felt strong and confident and made no apologies for what was coming out of our mouths. We've all had moments when we've said something and it felt like it just came out of our core and people just stopped and listened. If you go back and think about how it felt to speak powerfully, you'll find that it came from your guts or all the way down from your balls. Most likely it was as if an energy came up from that part of your body and out your mouth. We're going to teach you how to reproduce that experience at will.

Men who feel intimidated around talking to women cut off their life energy and their vitality. When you speak from your balls you feel more confident because you have your life energy supporting you. When you have vitality and confidence, talking to women is much easier.

The idea of speaking from your balls or your guts is not that unusual. We know that peak performers in sports and other fields incorporate this concept into their success strategies. They get really grounded in their guts or their balls; they feel a connection to that area, they breathe into it and they get psyched up. Peak performers use this practice to make themselves feel strong, confident and powerful before they go into a speech or important situation.

This is an awkward thing to discuss; the notion of coming from your balls is so foreign that our only connection to talking about it is to associate it with masturbation. We want you to start associating speaking from your balls with having the power to help you get what you want with women, not with something to feel embarrassed about or hide from.

Here's how you can use this energy. Start by closing your eyes and sensing the energy around your navel and your balls. We're not talking about jerking off here or anything like that—sense it internally. Sense that energy, sense your balls, and then breathe into it. Next, feel your breath circulate down to your guts and balls and then come back up. The more comfortable and familiar you become with that energy, the more confident you will feel with women. The more familiar you are with that energy, the easier it will be to access that sense of calm and confidence when you are talking to women. This simple practice can be done anytime, anywhere.

When they first start working with us, most of our students tend to speak from their heads or their throat. It's as if they are cut off below their necks. They don't feel powerful and instead avoid being grounded and in touch with their power. They are used to avoiding their balls and guts when they feel scared. You can train yourself, however, to focus on this area; over time, it will greatly enhance your self-confidence.

Breathing is an important aspect of learning to speak from your balls. It always sounds silly when someone tells you to breathe; if we weren't breathing, we'd be dead, obviously. But you can breathe deep down inside of yourself and imagine the air going deeply—or you can breathe shallowly. When men feel intimidated, they usually breathe shallowly. Breathing deeply helps you relax. Spend a few minutes each day breathing deeply into your navel and below, and feeling the power that comes from that part of your body.

Three Practices For Cultivating Vocal Excitement

Just as you need physical vitality, you also need to project vocal excitement. Here are a few practices to experiment with that will enhance your vocal capacity.

- Imagine that there's an excitement meter inside of you. When the meter is at ten, you are bursting with excitement; zero equals being dead. Most of the time shy men are around one or two on the excitement meter. They don't want to rock the boat or let things get out of control, so they don't get more excited. One way for you to get more excited is to put yourself in front of a mirror and see how close to 10 you can get. Try this for 30 seconds to a minute and see how it feels to have the excitement circulate through your body.

- Spend time with another person and take at least a minute to get more excited about something than you normally would be. You can go into this one step at a time; you don't have to peg it at 10 right away. If you're normally at one or two, let yourself go to four or five, then gradually raise the bar. This might seem crazy to you. In fact, it is silly, and when you're excited you risk looking silly. When you're in the flow of being excited, however, it's attractive to women. You can get away with a lot more when you're excited about something than you can when you're dull and boring.

  People want to be around excited people. If you're willing to accept your own enthusiasm about things, which might be silly, other people will also be okay with it. If you're willing to accept those silly parts of yourself, a woman will know that you will also accept her silly and awkward parts.

- Act excited about mundane things. You can choose to be excited about life or you can choose to be dead. You can hide in your house, be afraid to talk to anyone and be afraid to show your interest in anything, but this will only keep you further away from women. The alternative: get engaged in life and take the risks to let yourself engage with women. We're giving you permission to let yourself show your enthusiasm.

CONCLUSION

You now know The Hi Program, and how to implement it in your life. We invite you to decide to start using The Hi Program today. Chose how many women you are going to say hi to each day, and start doing it. Keep track. See what comes up to block you, get through those blocks, and celebrate your successes. The Hi Program is the foundation for taking the next steps with women we will teach you in upcoming chapters.

You also now know about creating and increasing physical and vocal vitality. Both of these factors will be important in you future abilities to converse seductively with women. •

How to Talk to Women

CHapter 3
THE Inner Game of Talking to Women

"If one advances confidently in the direction of his dreams, and endeavors to live the life which he has imagined, he will meet with a success unexpected in common hours."

—Henry David Thoreau

There is an inner game of talking to women. It's all about grappling with yourself and dealing with your fears at every stage of approaching and talking to women.

You might say that there is a war in your head. There's a battleground inside you. Perhaps there is a part of you that wants to talk to women while another part is scared to death of rejection. One part of you wants relationships with women; another part only wants short-term sex. One part of you feels strong and confident; another part of you feels scared and intimidated.

Let's spend some time looking at the internal struggles related to seduction and offering some tips on how to handle the inevitable internal problems that come up when approaching women.

Problems Men Have When Communicating With Women

Defending, apologizing and protecting yourself. When talking to women, many men feel as if they have to defend themselves. They immediately assume that everything a woman says is a personal attack. These men act as if women are out to get them, out to humiliate them, and the only thing they can do to retaliate is be prepared for an inevitable attack.

When Bob the bad seducer talks to women he is constantly on guard and wondering when she will attack him. He stares at her with an angry expression. When a woman asks him a personal question he takes on a defensive tone and says, "What do you mean by that?" or "Why do you think that's your business?" Bob is so wrapped up in his paranoia that he is unable to have a conversation with a woman.

Taking a defensive position when you're talking to women does not work. When you take on a defensive position and assume a woman is attacking you, being aggressive or trying to harm you, you seem uncomfortable, mean and nasty. You need to be open when you're talking to women. When you're focused on defending yourself or apologizing for your sexual interest you cannot listen to a woman and cannot have fun with her. When you're with a woman, look for times when you're defending and protecting yourself and times when you aren't. What's the difference? What are the internal triggers?

The other side of being defensive is being protective. What are you protecting yourself from when you're talking to women? Usually you are protecting yourself from rejection or from looking like a moron, or else you're simply trying too hard to look good. Unfortunately there is nothing you can do but take risks with women. You always risk looking stupid, being vulnerable and being awkward. Approaching women is inherently risky and vulnerable. You have to decide to live with it.

Another common trap is apologizing for your sexual interest. Shy men feel as though approaching women is wrong. They think that if they show romantic or sexual interest it in some way hurts a woman. These men think they are so powerful that they can ruin any woman's day merely by commenting that she is beautiful or showing any interest.

Strategizing. There are concrete skills you can learn to help you succeed with women. It's smart to study seduction materials; study this book and our other products and learn as much about yourself, women, romance and sexuality as possible. Studying, however, is all about preparation. Once you're having an actual conversation with a woman, all the rules change.

Once you're in an actual conversation with a woman it's best to try to forget about forcing an outcome; relax and have fun. To be in the present moment you need to give up any strategy that you may have.

There are a few reasons why strategizing does not work:

- The experience of being with women changes from moment to moment, so any strategy you employ will not be applicable to the inevitable curveballs women will throw at you. How can you have a strategy for a situation that has no predictability? You can't.

- Strategizing makes you blind to openings. When you are talking to women there are subtle openings to ask for phone numbers, initiate different types of conversations, go for the first kiss, and more. When you're focused solely on your strategy you will not see the openings for moving things further. You need to be in an odd Zenlike state of being immersed in the situation yet detached enough to see when to ask for her phone number. If you are solely focused on a strategy you'll miss the openings.

- Strategizing is not fun. Why do we keep talking about fun? Fun men turn women on. When you're having fun you're in the flow and when you're miserable and struggling you are not attractive. When you focus on a strategy and work hard to seduce women, you take all the fun out of it and make talking to women feel like work. Relax and find ways to enjoy the experience.

- Strategizing makes you come across as a freak. A man who is focused on a strategy comes across as awkward and uncomfortable. Telemarketers are always trying to use cute lines and stupid questions to engage you and they always come across as time wasters. Salesmen who have an agenda or are using a sales strategy come across as creepy. When you are focused on a strategy or using a technique you too will come across as superficial and creepy.

Think about how a martial artist goes into a fight. He works on his kicks, his punches, his blocks and more. He works for years developing muscles and strength, practicing in the dojo with his fellow students. During an actual fight he uses everything he's ever learned during his training. He uses the blocks, the kicks, the punches and more.

But to do that, during the actual fight he must give up any strategy and any skill he's learned and be aware of the other fighter. He must be open to responding to anything that happens. If he's focused on showing off, strategizing or expecting the other fighter to fight a particular way he's in for a rude awakening. The moment he starts thinking he understands how the fight will go he'll likely get his ass kicked. The moment he starts expecting a kick or a punch, the other fighter will do something completely different and knock him out. With women you need to let go of any strategy and skill you've learned and be open to whatever happens. When you can be aware, present and open, talking to women will be fluid and fun.

Manipulating. Do you want to learn a surefire method for feeling like a jerk? Do you want to find a way to feel guilty, crummy about yourself and regretful? Manipulating women is one way you can create a situation where you feel like a total jerk.

We've worked with thousands of men, and the number one concern they have in seducing women is that they want to date and have sex without being a jerk. Men tell us that when they manipulate and lie to women they feel terrible. They feel guilty and depressed. Men tell us that even when manipulation works the cost is not worth it. The ultimate cost for manipulating women is your self-esteem. Fortunately, you don't need to manipulate. You can build real connections, using the tools in this book.

Looking for certainty. If you want to learn to be a powerful seducer then you need to stop looking for certainty. If you are searching for a seduction method that is based on certainty and stability you will fail every time. Talking to women is all about uncertainty and unpredictability. Talking to women is like jumping off a high diving board. So what do you do? You can either climb back down or decide not to jump or you can muster up the courage to go for it. If you jump there are a few seconds in which you are falling through the air, which feels scary, exhilarating and intense.

Talking to women is like jumping off a diving board. At first there is no way of knowing how things will go. You don't know if she's got a boyfriend, if you're her type, if you'll offend her with a comment or if you'll take her home that night and have sex with her. To have a chance at success, however, you need to jump and go for it and understand that you have no clue about whether you'll succeed or fail. We all get scared when we first approach a woman. We all feel nervous and uncertain and doubt our skills. You can still go for it, though. Your job is to feel the fear and still do it anyway!

Resisting the truth. Many of our students have a hard time facing the harsh realities of dating women. Most men want a sanitized version of dating women; they want the version without the risk of pain and humiliation. Guess what? That's not real. Most women on this planet are not the slightest bit interested in dating you. So what? You're only looking for the handful of women who are.

Let's get honest here. Harsh truths that you must face:

- Some of our students meet women who have boyfriends and they will not accept the fact that the woman is already taken.
- Some of our students keep calling a woman even after a few dates have gone badly. They fail to accept the fact that the woman is not interested in them.
- Some of our students keep calling women even after a few dates have gone badly. They fail to accept that they don't like the woman!
- We all meet women we find attractive who have no interest in us.
- The vast majority of women you talk to are not interested in you.

It's important to see the truth and accept facts. When you hold on to false hopes and lie to yourself it's hard to succeed with women. Pain can be a great motivator. It's our belief that it's better to be honest and real, it's better to feel the pain of failure and loneliness, than it is to lie to yourself. The pain can become an ally, not something to resist. When you're able to be honest it's much easier to come up with an action plan and get back into the game of dating.

Forcing an outcome. As men, one way we succeed in life is by forcing outcomes. If you're a computer programmer, for instance, through sheer hard work, discipline and drive you can accomplish nearly anything and complete any project. If you're a doctor or an academic you can push yourself and struggle through medical school or struggle through your Ph.D. thesis process. You can push yourself at any job to work overtime, do additional studying, take on additional responsibilities and accomplish tasks you never thought you could.

Succeeding with women is different from success at work. When it comes to seducing women hard work is important, but hard work alone will not bring you success. You can control a lot of outcomes at work. You can't control women. You cannot control outcomes with women. None of us knows what a particular woman wants, what turns her on, what she's looking for in a man. So you cannot approach the issue of how to seduce women in the same way you would your work problems. With women it's all an experiment. You show up, run some communication experiments like Deepening Questions and Romantic Questions, and see what the response is like. If she's open you do some more, if she's unreceptive you move on.

This is also true when going on dates. You cannot force a woman to have sex with you or be in the mood to make out. You can show up and do your best to create a romantic mood. Then again, you can do everything perfectly and she still might not be turned on by you. The bottom line is twofold:

- You cannot control outcomes with women.
- You can only show up and do your best.

You cannot force outcomes with women. Do not even try.

Trying to solve her problems. Trying to solve a woman's problems is suicide. You might as well just put a gun to your head and blow your brains out if you think a woman will be romantically interested in you if you solve her problems.

Many men use the therapist ploy to attempt to become lovers with women. The ploy usually works this way: a guy is a friend with a woman he wants to date. He thinks that if she opens up to him emotionally then it will likely lead to sex. He thinks that if he can solve her emotional problems she will want to date him. Then, to his surprise, things pan out differently.

Lying. Some dating "experts" encourage men to lie to women as a way to get sex. We are wholly against lying to women and do not in any way encourage you to lie. We want you to cultivate the skills to create relationships with women you can feel good about, not regret.

What does lying say about you? Lying says that you are the kind of guy who cannot get women by being honest. You cannot get women unless you pretend you're someone else. You cannot get women if you are just you. Lying leads to a lack of self-respect and to regret.

Lying might work in the short term, but ultimately it's very costly. What if you end up really liking a woman and want to pursue a relationship with her? Then she finds you out you lied to her and she's no longer interested. What if you forget about the lies you told and a woman catches you in one of your lies? How is that going to go over? What if the word gets around that you're a liar?

The bottom line is that lying is unnecessary and tends to cause more problems than it's worth. Instead, we recommend you cultivate internal integrity and avoid lying to women.

Comparing yourself to other men. Rarely is it motivating to compare yourself to other men. This book and this program are about you and you alone. It's about what you can do to get women into your life. We all have different experiences and skills. What most of our students do is look at the bad boys, and the men who are with the hottest women, and feel jealous and depressed. Our students say things like:

- Other men are rich and can therefore easily get women.
- Other men live in a city with more hot women per capita.
- Other men have a job that is more conducive to meeting women.
- Other men are younger than I am and therefore have an easier time.
- Other men are taller.
- Other men are in better physical shape.
- Other men are just naturals.

All of these excuses are traps. There is nothing you can do about other men; all you can do is change yourself.

Rather than focusing on what other men are doing and all the lucky breaks they have, what can you do? Maybe you're very inexperienced with women and to you it's a huge stretch just to say hi to women. If that's hard for you then start by saying hi and build your skills from there. Other men feel more comfortable and need to start experimenting with the advanced conversational modes in this book. Some men may feel clueless about dating women and want to buy The Mastery Program audio course because they need a comprehensive program for meeting and dating women. (Check out our web site, www.howtosucceedwithwomen.com, for more information on that and other helpful products.) No matter where you are in the process, comparing yourself to other men is not useful. What's useful is constructing a plan of action that improves your skills.

Beating up on yourself. One key difference between successful seducers and unsuccessful seducers is that the most successful seducers don't beat themselves up. Instead, they constantly focus on the ways in which they are successful with women.

Dating women is a long-term project, and as with all long-term projects the goal is small incremental progress over time. Sometimes there will be big steps forward; sometimes, small steps backward. Along the way there will be upset, pain, harsh reality, scary moments, fun and joy. You need to develop an internal approach to see the positive steps you take with women. In the confusing, long odyssey of dating women, you need to constantly look at the movement and steps you've taken and constantly compliment and reward yourself for your own progress.

You can either look at each interaction with women and kick yourself for the ways you blew it or you can celebrate the fact that you actually did something. Unfortunately, beating up on yourself has become a way of life for many of our students. They make a practice out of feeling guilty for any opportunities they didn't take with women, errors they made while talking to women and opportunities to ask for phone numbers they didn't take. Instead, we recommend you keep track of all the things you do correctly. When you can see the things you've done correctly and the ways you've pushed yourself in new directions, it will enhance your self-confidence. If you only focus on the things you didn't do correctly you'll never improve.

Stop beating up on yourself or Louis & Copeland will break your finger! If beating up on yourself worked we'd tell you.

Not listening. To be an effective seducer it's important to develop listening skills. When you are able to listen carefully to what a woman says you learn important information about her. You learn what she likes and dislikes. You learn what she considers romantic and what she's passionate about. You also learn how to move the conversation into more seductive depths. These details are useful in coming up with date ideas and also in creating more rapport between the two of you.

All too often men don't listen to women because they're thinking about the next step in a seduction or maybe just the next question to ask. Deal with your internal dialog when you are talking to a woman and you will be able to pay attention to her.

Being on the couch and wishing you were out flirting with women. It's easy to sit on the couch at home wanting to interact with women. We all get frustrated and depressed and just do not want to go out and practice our seduction skills. But there is no other way to get women. They are not going to parachute into your backyard. They are not going to suddenly knock on your door and beg for sex. They are not going chase you down the street and then take off their shirt and beg you to feel them up then and there. It just ain't gonna happen.

Here's how we recommend you change this pattern: get up, leave the house and go anywhere other than home.

Perhaps your eventual goal is to go to bars and talk to women, but at the moment you're terrified of doing so. Instead, you can start tonight by going to bookstores and saying hi to 10 women. If you're home on the couch, see if you can get motivated to take one small step toward talking to women by leaving your house. Maybe you'll just go to the coffee shop and smile at a few women. That's a much bigger step than staying at home.

Scamming women. Remember the line from the movie *Body Heat* about the perfect crime? "A hundred things can go wrong with every 'perfect crime.' If you're a genius, you can think of 50 of them. And you're not a genius." Do guys who use transparent scams to get women actually think women are dumb enough to fall for them? We know a hot young bisexual female who spends a lot of time online. She says it's not shocking that men try to scam on her online—it's just shocking how transparent these scams usually are.

The bottom line is this: most of the time when you think you're getting away with something, you're actually being incredibly obvious. This makes people—especially women—hate you and not want to give you what you want.

Many of us learned early on in life that the only way to get ahead is to scam people. It's either be a scam artist or get nothing at all—or, even worse, be screwed by everybody else scamming you. The problem with this is that while scamming may get some results occasionally, it costs you your self-respect and self-esteem as a man. Scamming is what a guy does when he's looking for a quick fix for life's problems, and quick fixes never work in the long term. How does a guy feel about himself after trying some lame pickup line or routine on a woman and having her throw her drink in his face? How does a guy feel about himself when he spends $50 on pheromone cologne and it has no effect on women?

Often guys with a scam orientation think that it's almost a duty to take as much as they can from people. If you give them an inch, they try to take a mile. If they can get a mile, they go for even more. If you are like this, women you try to scam on will sense it and avoid you. Businesses you try to scam will catch you. Scams are hard on your self-respect. Even when they work, they reinforce the idea that you have to scam to get by in life, and that has a psychological cost.

Men are famous for confusing kindness for blindness. Just because a woman is nice doesn't mean she won't hit back if you try to scam on her. The belief that you can or should take people for all you can get ultimately does not work with women or for getting the life you want. If you want something from someone, you've got to make an effort to build a mutually beneficial connection. You must create positive flirting conversations that give women good feelings and make them want to see you again.

What's really needed is to get out of the entire scam orientation. A seducer who isn't a scam artist understands that paying the price is what it's all about. Such a man just wants to know what the price is. He isn't trying to pull a fast one. This shows up with women in learning how to make a real, human, romantic connection, even if your goal is a short-term sexual relationship.

Benjamin Franklin once said, "If rascals knew the pleasure of virtue, they would become virtuous out of sheer rascality." When you work the fundamentals and build connections with people—what Franklin might call being virtuous—you really can get what you want.

Not asking for the number or stepping up the seduction. Seize opportunities when they are in front of you! Opportunities are there for one reason: for you to take them. Yes it's true, if you fail to take opportunities life will not end, and you shouldn't beat yourself up. At the same time, the world of talking to women is all about creating bigger and bigger openings to risk taking things to the next level. Perhaps you want to talk to a woman and you risk talking to her; the next risk is asking her out. Push yourself to take the next risk. Push yourself to go for it. When an opportunity shows up, go for it, rather than regret not going for it later.

Only trying one approach or experimenting with one technique or niche. If you use only one technique in this book, you will fail. Successful seduction is built on a foundation of experimentation. You never know with any degree of certainty what will eventually work. You need to experiment with online dating, meeting women in bars, trying many different niches and constantly being on the lookout for new places to find women. You must try a variety of different approaches.

Letting your anger and frustration at women come through in your communication. It can be very frustrating to be out in the world risking and talking to women. It can be stressful, scary and downright aggravating. It's very frustrating to walk down the street and see so many hot women and feel like you have no shot with them. It's frustrating to see other men have the success you want.

The solution is to create spaces where you can let out your frustration— spaces where there are no women around.

If you are a guy who gets frustrated easily, and many of us do, you need to find outlets for that frustration. If you come across as an angry man to women they will not only be turned off by you, they will most likely find you intimidating and want to avoid you. You need to understand your frustration enough to see when it's coming out with women. If you are a nice guy you may come across as arrogant and mean.

Here's how you come can come across as angry to women:

- Seeming snotty
- Seeming judgmental
- Seeming dismissive
- Seeming like you are lecturing people
- Saying things that seem like roundabout ways of telling people to shut up
- Joking around in ways that seem condescending or patronizing
- Being sarcastic in ways that seem mean

This does not mean you have to walk on eggshells around women and act like you are Mr. Happy all the time. It means you act respectfully and do not come across as a mean guy.

SOLUTIONS

Be authentic. We've already talking about being self-expressed and having character. Women want a man who is interesting and interested. You need to find your edge, the parts of yourself that are unique. Women want a man with passion and energy. Look at how you can express yourself with women and show your character.

Have fun. Fun attracts more fun. Depression attracts more depression; fear attracts more fear. Women want to be around fun men. One reason comedians get women, even though many comedians are not particularly attractive, is because they are fun to be around. Women find men who make them laugh or are fun to be around sexy and exciting— in other words, potential lovers. For many women playfulness, fun and sexiness are linked. Have fun and make every interaction fun for both of you.

Give up how it has to look. When you're dealing with women you need to give up your ideas of how a conversation or interaction should look. You never know what will happen. Maybe you end up talking to a woman at a concert and you get her number but don't bring her home. Maybe a woman seems really into you but never calls you back. Maybe she's only interested in you as friend and not a lover. You will not find this out unless you give up your preconceived notions of how it should look, and find out what really is there. You have no clue what the relationship will look like. And since you cannot control the interaction or her interest level, all you can do is show up and go with the flow.

By going with the flow we don't mean being totally passive and not trying to move things into a more seductive realm; you should take risks to make things as seductive as possible. But if you are too focused on getting a number/email address or having an interaction look a particular way you will miss the direction she wants things to go. You will miss the cues she's giving you and openings to take the interaction deeper.

It's a paradox. At one point you need to give up any attachment and any focus on what things need to look like. At the other you need to try to push things into more romantic spaces. Be cognizant of both of these approaches and do your best to stay in between both.

Cut off communication and avoid people and situations that make you uncomfortable. Sometimes you need to cut a date short and leave. A man who has self-respect does not stay in situations where he feels condescended to, obligated to pay for things that don't feel right or offended or otherwise made uncomfortable by a woman.

Once again we're not talking about being rude or mean, but sometimes dates are not going well and even feel really bad. We're giving you permission to leave these situations and go somewhere else. You do not need to subject yourself to women and situations that feel bad. You will likely end up talking to and dating women who you're not into being around. In those situations the best tactic is to leave when there's an opportunity to do so.

Stay in communication with friends and buddies. One of the best ways to increase your skills with women is to have a buddy you can talk to about how your seduction experiments are going. A buddy is good because you can call him for support bounce ideas off of him.

Having someone you can talk to about women on a regular basis is very helpful in staying motivated, pushing yourself and overcoming trouble. You will also learn a lot about yourself by being a buddy to another man in helping him date women.

Focus on your goals and keep your word to yourself about approaching and saying hi to women. You need to come up with a seduction plan. This means you have goals, both short and long-term. This means you come up with a strategy to practice talking to women. Perhaps you commit to saying hi to 10 women per day, practicing the Romantic Moves a few times per week and having at least two Deepening Conversations (all of which you will learn later in this book). Whatever your goals are you need to push yourself to keep your word.

Unsuccessful seducers don't take their promises seriously and blow off accomplishing their goals. Successful seducers keep their word no matter what. If they promise to talk to a certain number of women each day or week, they do it.

Make it into a game. Talking to women is a game. Yes, there are emotional components to dealing with women; yes, it feels like your ego is on the line oftentimes, but it's only a game. It's not real. It's not a matter of life and death. There are no real consequences.

So how can you shift the focus from being serious and heavy to having fun and enjoying the game? You can start tracking your progress, doing things just for the hell of it, checking things out knowing it's not that serious and creating your own rules.

Dance in the conversation. Have you had the experience where you were talking to someone and time just seemed to stand still and the next thing you knew hours had passed? In those moments you were in the flow, you were dancing in the conversation. You were open and free and just really synched up with the other person. So how do you replicate that experience? There is no clear path to doing it every day or at will. Just be open to dancing in a conversation today. The goal is to have fluidity in your communication.

Have self-respect. The problem with damaging your self-respect to pursue a woman is that it is self-reinforcing: the more your betray your own self-respect and grovel to a woman, the more likely you are to betray yourself again the next time. To make matters worse, when you violate your self-respect with a woman, it arouses her contempt for you, and she will treat you even worse. If you stay around for that, she'll hurt you even more. You'll be left wondering why you—such a nice, understanding guy—are caught up with a woman who treats you so badly. It will all be because you sold your self-respect for sex, which is a bad deal and almost never actually gets you the girl.

This doesn't mean you should be mean to a woman, go crazy or do anything else that would damage your self-respect. You just have to decide where the line is and live with it intelligently.

Be experimental. You never know what will work for you until you try it. Part of being experimental is trying new things. Be open to trying new things rather than dismissing them beforehand. Being experimental means you realize that you need to go through a bunch of interactions before one works so you might as well try a bunch of stuff in the meantime.

Perhaps you check out "speed dating" or you answer a personal ad, just to check it out. Maybe you check out a new place where you might meet women, or a yoga class—anything out of the norm. The most successful seducers are always trying out new things, coming up with new approaches, checking out new social opportunities and experimenting with new approaches.

Trust your gut. You need to start trusting yourself when you interact with women. We say that when you're attracted to a woman and feel some spark between the two of you, trust that. Trust your intuition with women. Trust your gut when dealing with women in all phases of seduction. When a situation doesn't feel right get out of it. If you meet a woman and something about the interaction feels off, trust that feeling. Trust yourself.

Add urgency. One of the differences between successful and unsuccessful seducers is that successful ones have urgency in their seductions. Successful seducers have a gutsy quality about their lives where they play full-out and realize that this could be their one and only opportunity to seduce a particular woman. Urgency means you go for it, you move quickly and deliberately. You act swiftly and cut to the chase. You go for it. You jump in. You bypass the doubts and the excuses and just do it.

This is not a practice life; this is the real thing. Adding urgency means you ask her out, you approach her rather than worry about it, you ask for her number, you make the call rather than procrastinate, you get out and practice, you add a little more do-or-die quality to your life with women.

A Few Rules Of Women

We've noticed that many of our students are frustrated because they expect women to act the way men do, and to be motivated in the same way men are. To help correct this, we've put together this list of the rules of women.

These rules are generalizations; you will, of course, find women who are exceptions to all of them. Don't worry about it. The bottom line is, your interactions with women will go more easily if you act as though these rules are true.

Women are not screwed-up men. Women are not just screwed-up or illogical men. They are women. If you relate to women as if they were just screwed-up men, you'll always be trying to make women act the way you wish they would act—that is, the way you would act.

Women have a different integrity from men. While men are more likely to have integrity to their word, women are more likely to have integrity to their feelings. This means that if a woman's feelings tell her to do something that is contrary to what she said she'd do, such as showing up for a date, she's likely to do what her feelings tell her to rather than to follow her commitment. Another way to say this is to say that women are, on the whole, more committed to doing what their emotions tell them than they are to keeping their word. Don't let this drive you crazy. It's not bad, just different from the way you are.

Women want to be free to change their minds. Women want to be able to change their minds as much as they want whenever they want for whatever reason they want or for no reason at all. This may seem crazy or illogical to you, but remember—she's following her feelings, not her verbal commitments.

Women use hints and innuendoes to tell you what they want. When you interact with women, don't expect them to be direct with you about what they want. Once again, this isn't being screwed-up, it's just a difference in the ways men and women do things. This means that when you ask women what they want you should provide a menu of options rather than expecting them to generate ideas.

Women want life to be an unending date. Women want things to be romantic. In some ways they prefer an emotional roller-coaster to a smooth ride. Another way to say this is to say that women have a wide emotional range and want to express it fully.

Women can be surprisingly mean. Many men who've gone through a divorce have found out how surprisingly mean women can be. In some ways this is because women are more invested in the concept of fairness than men are. While you don't expect life to be fair and don't think about it much, the women in your life very well might. So if you feel shafted, you might not do much about it...but if a woman feels shafted, often she feels it's only fair for her to even the score and take revenge.

Women want what they want when they want it because they want it. Asking a woman why she wants something—or, even worse, why she doesn't—is always a mistake. She wants it because she wants it. Which, when you think about it, is basically true for you too. Give her the space to want what she wants when she wants it because she wants it and don't let it drive you crazy if it doesn't make sense to you.

CONCLUSION

If you are really going to effectively use the tools in this book, you have to have a sense of how to handle the "inner game" of talking to women, as well as the skill-based "outer game" of talking to them. You have to be able to handle the challenges provided by your own issues with women, and your own fears. In this chapter you have started that process. In the next chapter, you'll learn how to handle fear of rejection and panic. Once you have those handled, you'll be in a great place for beginning to talk to women. •

CHAPTER 4

HANDLING REJECTION AND PANIC AROUND WOMEN

By this point, you may have started The Hi Program. If you have, how is it going, interrupting women by saying hi to them? Is it hard or easy? Are you taking opportunities or not? Are you starting to see that there are a lot of women around you all the time whom you usually tune out and ignore? Are you seeing opportunities and purposefully not taking them? Or are you one of those guys who says, "Well, saying hi to women is going to be really easy. In fact, it's so easy that I'll put it off till tomorrow."

Not saying hi and not interrupting women because it's too easy is a fairly standard scam. Just realize that saying hi may be more intimidating than you thought. Accept that fact, stop making excuses and go and say hi to some women.

Interrupting women by saying hi, asking her a question or using any other method will have at least one certain consequence: some percentage of the time you will experience rejection. This probably doesn't come as such a huge shock, does it? You were probably thinking about it before this point: "Wait a minute—if I say hi to women and interrupt them, they'll shoot me down!" Interrupting women, while it does lead to success, will also inevitably lead to some rejection. It could be painful!

The problem with avoiding pain by never interacting with women is that you end up with a life in which you are depressed and lonely and (paradoxically) end up feeling rejected all the time anyway! So it makes sense to learn how to handle rejection so you can minimize or even obliterate the impact it has on you and thus interact more freely with women. This chapter will give you concrete actions and steps you can take to deal with rejection powerfully. This tool for handling rejection is simple but it has dramatically changed our lives. Being able to handle rejection is the oil that lubricates our system for talking to women. You must learn how to use it.

Learning to talk to and seduce women is a process, and each step of that process you risk rejection. When you interrupt women and say hi, you risk rejection. When you flirt with women, you risk rejection. When you conduct Romantic Conversations, you risk rejection. When you ask for a woman's phone number and email address, you risk rejection. When you ask a woman for a Priming Date, you risk rejection. When you go on a Priming Date, you risk rejection. When you go for a first kiss, you risk rejection. When you go for more, you risk rejection. Every step of the way, you are risking rejection with women.

To make matters worse, as you learn how to talk to women, you are likely to be rejected at every step in the process at one time or another. When you first start interrupting and saying hi to women, you are likely to feel stopped by the women who reject your interruptions. In time, you will get through that and get into conversations with women. You will try the Flirting Moves; sometimes they'll work, other times they'll be rejected. Get through that and start showing your romantic interest and conducting

Romantic Conversations; sometimes you'll experience rejection there too. At every step—getting her number, asking her out, going for that first kiss, all of it—you will sometimes experience rejection. Knowing how to handle it and how to keep moving forward, even in the face of fear of rejection, is critical.

Because seduction is a numbers game, you'll want to move through a lot of women to get to the eventual yeses that you want. You'll want to move through those nos, those rejections, as quickly and efficiently as you can while keeping your spirits high. Since we developed this tool, we've been able to laugh in the face of rejection (at least some of the time), deal with it and move on without it being a big problem (almost all of the time). You must be able to do this, too.

We make a lot of appearances on radio and TV call-in shows and we receive email from a lot of men. The number one question we get is "How do I handle rejection?" Here's how you can do it the way that top seducers do.

HOW SUCCESSFUL AND UNSUCCESSFUL SEDUCERS HANDLE REJECTION

Let's compare how men who consistently fail with women handle rejection with how rejection is handled by men who succeed with women. There's a fundamental difference.

First, let's take a look at how guys who fail with women handle rejection and the fear of rejection. When Bob the bad seducer is rejected by a woman, the first thing he does is make that woman into his "one-and-only hope" of ever having sex again. He does this by idealizing her: "She was so pretty, and I never get to meet women like her. She had the whole package—great body, awesome tits, brains, a successful career. She really could have been 'the one'!"

The second thing Bob does is decide that her rejection of him is his fault. He'll tell himself, "She rejected me because I'm so ugly and I'm stupid. What makes me think I'd be attractive to a woman like her, anyway? I'm not attractive. All I am is a piece of shit. I know that. Plus, what I said to her was incredibly stupid. I really handled it wrong. I really freaked her out. I should just crawl back into my hole and die. I'll never succeed with women. Why do I always have such bad luck with women? I suck."

But wait—there's more! After eviscerating himself in step two, Bob, and unsuccessful seducers like him, takes another key step toward using this rejection to keep himself from ever taking a risk with a woman again: he wallows in the pain of it. That's right, after making the woman into "the perfect woman" and making the rejection completely his own fault and coming up with an explanation for the rejection that is as painful as he can devise, brilliant Bob dwells in that pain.

He replays the experience of being rejected over and over, giving himself a new dose of emotional pain every time he relives it. He imagines the look on her face when she rejected him and thinks how upset she must have been. He tells himself that she no doubt convened a meeting of all of her friends just to talk about the trauma that Bob put her through. He imagines that his reputation, such as it was, is ruined. He tells himself that now "everyone will know" he was trying to be a seducer—and it's all because he bungled things so badly.

And then Bob wonders why it takes him four months to get up the nerve to approach another woman, and why talking to women is so incredibly hard.

Sure, this is an extreme example. But the weird thing is that it's not all that unusual. We've known many men who do this—and worse!—to themselves on a regular basis. Heck, we even used to be such guys. If either of us asked a woman out and she said no, or if either of us tried to kiss a woman and she said, "Oh, I only like you as a friend," we'd go into the whole "I suck, she was so pretty" routine. We'd make her our one-and-only hope, then say, "If only I were more attractive or luckier or smarter or richer" or whatever… Then we'd dwell in the pain for days and use that "failure" to make it even harder to approach women again.

Just the other day we talked to a guy who had this problem. He told us about how he went ballroom-dancing a month ago and a woman there rejected him. This was a month ago and he was still recreating the pain of it, over and over, on a daily basis. He can't even approach other women because he's too busy reliving the pain of that one rejection. You've probably done this too.

People naturally think that they need to know they can survive whatever life might throw at them. So in order to be safe, when a woman rejects a man, part of him wants to make that rejection as bad as possible so

that he knows he can survive it no matter how bad it gets. People cata-
strophize rejection and make it much worse than it is to see if they can
make it through. You are probably doing the same thing when you try
to make sure you can survive the worst possible explanation about why
a woman may have rejected you.

Catastrophizing probably comes naturally to human beings. Think about
it. Which of our ancestors were more likely to survive—the ones who
never worried about anything or the ones who worried constantly about
things that could go wrong and who made sure they were ready for any
bad thing that might come along? Obviously, the ancestors who worried
about possible future problems had an edge on those who never worried.

The same principle does not hold true when it comes to rejection. Those
who put themselves through the pain of rejection over and over don't
have an edge on the men who don't think about rejection. It's unnecessary and it doesn't help the slightest bit in getting you what you want
with women. It's like Mark Twain said: "I've suffered many horrible misfortunes, most of which never happened." You don't need to have a life
of horrible misfortunes that never happened. Just because you can make
something bad emotionally doesn't meet that you should. You are not
obligated to do so just to prove that you can survive it. Knowing this will
help a lot in the area of rejection.

One of the main reasons that talking to women is so difficult for most
men is that they've created so much emotional pain—thanks to their way
of handling rejection—that when they think about risking with women

they can only feel all that pain. Once you're able to reverse that process and have experiences of being rejected that aren't upsetting, it will be much easier to initiate more with women—and to have more success.

Now let's look at rejection through the eyes of a successful seducer.

When a successful seducer like Bruce encounters rejection, he also follows a three-step process, albeit a different one from Bob's. When Bruce encounters rejection, the first thing he does is remind himself that dating is a numbers game and that in no way is this woman his one-and-only hope. Statistically, whatever you do with a woman is probably going to fail anyway because that's just life. He says this to himself: "Great. That's one more no I don't have to hear on my way to an inevitable yes."

Second, Bruce comes up with an explanation of her rejection that does not make it his fault. Specifically, he creates an explanation for the rejection that is because of her, not because of him. He may say to himself, "She must be a lesbian" or "She must be ill" or "Maybe her dog just died." It doesn't matter what it is as long as it's something that his brain can latch on to that isn't catastrophic and that doesn't involve him.

Let's spend a few moments talking about this step because it is so important and so hard for a lot of the men we work with. Just because an explanation is horribly negative and painful doesn't mean you are required by law to believe it. The truth is you have no clue why she rejected you. Maybe she was in a hurry. Maybe her cat died. Maybe she doesn't speak English. You don't know, and it doesn't serve you to believe the worst possible explanation. Make up something positive! It really is just as likely to be true as some horrible explanation that's all about you.

Guys so often think that they are all-knowing and omnipotent. But the truth is you are not the center of a woman's universe; she is the center of her universe. The reasons why she does things are more likely to be about her than about you. But it's incredibly common for a guy to think that a woman's world is about him. He'll tell himself, "I know why she didn't say hi back. She could tell that I'm a bad guy, that I just want to get in her pants and I'm only interested in sex." Meanwhile, the guy isn't important enough to the woman for her to spend her processing cycles on all these details about him. She's just trying to make it through the day, she has incredible cramps, her feet hurt, she's mad at her boss or whatever.

Believe it or not, the woman who rejected you does have a life outside of you. And that life is much more likely to be the reason that she rejected you than is her ability and inclination to see into your soul and divine what a scummy guy you are. She's just not that interested in you. She has problems of her own.

DAVID: I'm thinking about a time a few years ago when I thought I was rejected by a woman. I said hi to her and made some other remark and she just totally blew me off. She ignored me completely and walked away. I was left thinking that I must have done something wrong. I felt like a total worthless bum. I mentioned this incident to a friend of hers who asked me, "Were you on her left?" I said yes, I was. He said, "Well, she's very hard of hearing in general and can't hear in her left ear at all. I always make sure to be on her right when I'm talking to her." It turned out she hadn't heard me! The "rejection" had nothing to do with me at all. I thought, "Why didn't I come up with that explanation?"

You must not make this mistake. You must come up with an explanation for the rejection that is not about you. Let's say that again: You must come up with an explanation that is not about you. Make it her problem. Make it a problem with the environment. It doesn't matter—just make it a problem that has nothing to do with you.

Imagine you said hi to the woman at the grocery store. She didn't say hi back. What are some explanations that have nothing to do with you? "She just got stabbed with a pencil in her leg." "She's suffering from amnesia." "She just got out of the hospital." "She's been here since 5 a.m. and is exhausted." "She's having her period." It doesn't matter. Come up with some explanation. One that works really well is "Oh, I guess she's just really in her own world." Usually it's true. Usually women are just caught up in their own world—after all, everyone is.

Now to the third and final step. After Bruce reminds himself that dating is a numbers game and that she wasn't his one-and-only hope and after he comes up with an explanation for her behavior that has nothing to do with him, he redirects his focus toward something empowering.

Once again, you are not required by law to dwell in your suffering and experience the pain of rejection over and over again just because you can. Smart seducers think about something else—anything else. Pick up a newspaper, listen to the radio, go watch TV, go on a walk, go flirt with another woman—do something, but do it instantaneously, and let yourself get into doing it. The longer you wait, the more likely it is you will dwell in your pain. You've got to keep moving.

One great attention-redirecting question is "What do I want to do right now?" Often this question will help refocus the energy of the rejection into some activity that is useful to you. One man we know was flirting online with a woman whom he had previously had sex with and whom he was hoping to get into bed with again. At one point in their Instant Message conversation, she started telling him about this new guy she had met and about how he had come over for a night of hot sex the evening before.

Naturally, he felt rejected. So first he reminded himself that dating is a numbers game and that this woman was not his one-and-only hope. Second, he made the rejection her problem by explaining to himself that she was a very unstable alcoholic (which was true) and was probably drunk right then. Third, he redirected his attention by asking himself, "What do I want to do right now?"

He realized that he wanted to stop talking to this woman and answer some personals ads. So that's what he did. He was able to use the energy of the rejection to advance his whole seduction system, and it worked. He stopped thinking about the rejection and got into thinking about new opportunities with women.

The important thing is that you redirect your attention to something specific. It's not enough to tell yourself, "Don't think about the rejection" without putting some other activity into its place. You need to think about something specific or you'll just end up thinking about the rejection you aren't supposed to be thinking about. Find something else to focus on.

You probably know a guy who does all this automatically. He seems impervious to rejection. When you're at a bar with him, you notice that nothing stops him. After he's rejected by a woman, he'll say to you, "Oh well, she threw a drink in my face—I guess I'm on to the next one. Ha ha!" You've probably wondered how he did it. Well, this is how. He remembers it's a numbers game and that that rejection was just one more no he didn't have to hear again on his way to the inevitable yes. He makes the rejection her problem and then redirects his attention by moving on to the next woman (or anything else). Thus he eventually succeeds.

Remember that you have to do all three steps; you can't just do the one you like the best. Let's go over these three steps one more time and then give you some more examples:

- Remind yourself that dating is a numbers game and that this woman was not your one-and-only hope for sex. Remember that this is one more no on the way to the inevitable yes.
- Create an explanation for the rejection that has nothing to do with you. Make it a problem with her or a problem with the environment but not a problem with you.
- Redirect your attention. Find something else to think about or do. Ask yourself, "What do I want to do right now?" to give yourself ideas for things you can use the energy from the rejection to do.

Examples

Now let's look at some examples of Ron and David coaching each other as each pretends to have some trouble with this process.

DAVID: So, what happened?

RON: I was eating lunch and I went up to this woman behind the counter who was really hot. I said, "Hi, my name is Ron, how are you doing?" And she just turned away and she didn't talk to me. She just went and did something else.

DAVID: Did you tell yourself that it's a numbers game?

RON: Right, I could have done that. I could say to myself, "Hey, dating is a numbers game. It's not like there aren't 20 women in this place right now. I got upset because this one didn't work out—I don't need to do that. Also, that's just one more rejection I don't have to experience again on the way to the inevitable yes."

DAVID: What was the first thing that you did? Did you blame yourself or what?

RON: I thought, well, jeez, she's so hot, why isn't she talking to me? I must have blown it in some way. Did I say the wrong thing? Am I a jerk? What happened?

DAVID: So there's a way in which you blamed yourself and made the reason for the rejection about you. What are some of the reasons why she might have totally blown you off that have nothing to do with you? Just generate some of those.

RON: Well, obviously she was working, so perhaps she had some work to do. That might have been one possibility. Or perhaps she was in a hurry, or maybe she's not supposed to talk to customers. Or she may not have felt very good—it was the afternoon, maybe she was tired—or perhaps she was just in her own world.

DAVID: Great. How about the third step, which is redirecting your attention? Did you find yourself just naturally going over it again and again in your head?

RON: Yeah, I did at first. So I decided to change my focus instantaneously—to read the paper, eat a bagel—to do whatever there was to put my attention on. I interrupted the bad feeling as quickly as possible.

Do you get what we're talking about here? This really is about learning a "mental move." This is not just something theoretical. This is something actual that can dramatically change your life.

Now let's watch Ron coach David through the rejection process.

RON: So, tell me what happened.

DAVID: I went on a date with this girl. She was real pretty; I really liked her. We had another date planned, but she sent me an email saying she's still really in love with her ex-boyfriend and she's gone back to him and they are living together again and she doesn't want to go out with me after all. She said she hoped we could still be friends.

RON: Hmm, nothing cruel about that, eh? So first of all—what was the first thing that you did?

DAVID: I thought, "God, you know, that was such a pretty girl and we went on that date and the date went so well and she had so much cleavage and I loved her hair and there really aren't that many women who really are that pretty."

RON: So you started beating up on yourself.

DAVID: Yeah, like she was that "one-and-only hope."

RON: So, you failed to remember that it's a numbers game. What about the next step? What happened next?

DAVID: I could have said, "Of course! Statistically, that's gonna happen a certain amount of time. That's the kind of thing that happens in seducing. That's one more no I don't have to hear on the way to yes. I got pretty far with her, let's see what's next."

RON: What did you make it mean? What was your interpretation? Why did she send you this email?

DAVID: Well, that's because she couldn't even bear to see my face. I'm so hideous that I drove her back to her ex-boyfriend! I knew this would happen! This always happens to me! Why does this sort of thing always happen to me? Why don't women like me? I'm just not lovable. I'll never have the girl I want! All I can have is fat women! I suck!

RON: Okay, okay—everybody is feeling sick now! Now change the interpretation. What would be some other reasons why she did that?

DAVID: Well, she's really mixed up right now. Maybe she is really in love with her ex-boyfriend. That doesn't have anything to do with me. What am I going to do, go knock him off or something? Maybe she is really confused. And you know what? She wasn't that hot! It's not like there aren't hundreds and thousands of women around who are that hot and hotter! She's not that hot a commodity.

RON: Okay, cool. So the third part of it—did you dwell on it?

DAVID: So, dwelling on it. Yeah—moaning and thinking about it over and over and telling all my friends about this horrible rejection... But what I could have done was say, "Great, what do I want to focus on right now? How can I take some of the energy I've got right now and put it to use?"

RON: So long as you redirect your energy in some way.

DAVID: Yeah, just doing this I feel much better, more energized.

You need to retrain yourself to handle rejection properly. We have done this to the point where it is automatic. When we get rejected, our brains immediately respond because we have been working on it for years.

Percentages and Probabilities

DAVID: One thing that we have found to be incredibly helpful in dealing with the inevitability of a certain amount of rejection is putting a percentage likelihood on anything that may happen. Say Ron is getting ready to go out for a date and I say, "What do you think the odds are that you are going to have sex with her tonight?" and he says, "Oh, 20 or 30 percent" or something like that. Or say you're going out on a Priming Date and ask yourself, "What do you think the odds are that she's going to show up?" The answer might be something like "Oh, I give it about 70 percent."

For some reason, putting percentages on things seems to create some kind of "reality conversation" around them. You might say, "Great, there's a woman across the bar. There's a five percent probability that I could end up having sex with her tonight. That's one in 20—all I need is 20 her and I'm golden!" It makes it easier to approach a woman and less of a problem if things don't work out. Hey, there was a five percent chance; no big deal that it didn't work out. And a cause for celebration when it does!

Percentages and probabilities are another way to boil your interaction with a woman down to something tangible. So instead of it being this whole big scary thing, you say, "Well, look—there's a 10 percent chance it will go. No big deal."

DAVID: Yep, with that girl I was telling you about, I gave it a 50-50 chance that she would go back to her ex-boyfriend, because of the way that she was talking about him. That's what occurred. Those are the numbers. That's the game. It makes the task of relating to women easier.

Very often guys start out overly optimistic about their chances, so they're even more devastated if the interaction doesn't work out. They think, "Great, I have a 90 percent chance with that woman across the bar." Well, you almost never have a 90 percent chance with a woman. You must make a more realistic probability statement.

We use this tool in every area of our lives. What are the odds of us getting this new book deal? Say we think it's 40 percent. If so, all we need is a little more than possible deals and it'll be likely that we'll have a deal going. This is something for you to play around with. It may be useful for you to assign probabilities to things just to make different areas of your life clearer and more like a game.

Practicing the Rejection Process

The best way to become expert at handling rejection is to practice the rejection process. If you are doing the Hi Program (you are doing the Hi Program, aren't you?), it will give you a laboratory in which to experiment with the rejection process. When women don't say hi back or when they scowl or give you any other response that you consider a rejection, practice the rejection process. First, remind yourself that it's a numbers game and that this is one more no you don't have to hear again on your way to the eventual yes. Second, come up with an explanation for the rejection that has to do with her, not you. And third, redirect your attention, perhaps by asking yourself, "What do I want to do right now?"

Here are some tips for learning the process:

Write it down. It really helps if you write down the rejection process as you do it. The reason it's important to write it down is that doing it in your head is deceptive, especially at first. It's easy to do a sloppy and incomplete job if you are just thinking your way through the three-step process. You will think you have done the process, but you actually will not have—you will have thought about doing it, which your mind will misinterpret as having actually gone through the process for real. Writing down the rejection process gets it out of the realm of the abstract and into the realm of the real.

You may want to carry around a pen and some paper so that you can grab a minute or two and write down the process as you go through your day. Some of our students do the process in their heads during the day and then spend five minutes in the evening writing down and clarifying what they did in their heads earlier. Some men set aside a couple of minutes twice a day to write down their processes.

After you've written it down a number of times, you won't need to write it down so much anymore, although we still write it down on occasions when rejections seem to get to us more than they ought to.

Practice before you make the approach. Of course, you don't have to wait to experience rejection to use this process. You can also use it when you are thinking about approaching a woman and you feel the fear of rejection trying to stop you. Tell yourself, "If this doesn't go the way I want it to, I simply have to remember that dating is a numbers game and that this will be one more no on the way to my eventual yes. So even if she says no to me, this interaction will get me closer to my goal. Also, if she rejects me, it will probably be because she is in her own world or has a headache today or something like that. If she doesn't work out, I'll go talk to that other woman over there. Piece of cake, I'm ready to go!" This will prime your brain and put the interaction in perspective. So what if it doesn't work? Eventually one (and more) will.

Do it daily. As with any skill, it is much easier to master handling rejection if you practice the three-step process on a daily basis. If you say hi to a woman and she ignores you, do the three-step process. If you flirt with a woman and it doesn't go well, do the three-step process. If you ask a woman out for coffee and she says no, do the three-step process. If you go for the first kiss and she says she just wants to be friends, do the three-step process. You need to practice and have it be so ingrained in your mind that you just do it any time you need to. This will keep you going and keep you from getting stuck, and that is all that matters.

Do it until you get results. Oftentimes if you use the rejection process thoroughly you will feel completely better. Sometimes you'll feel 90 percent better or even only 50 percent better. That's all okay—it's moving in the right direction, and that's what's important.

What is not acceptable is doing the rejection process and feeling zero percent, one percent or two percent better. You aren't done with the process until you feel substantially better and have some energy to move on to something else. If you find you don't feel better, go through the process again. Remind yourself that dating is a numbers game; really feel how you've just heard one more no that you'll never need to hear again. Come up with new, more compelling reasons that make the rejection her problem, not yours. Find something that you really want to do and that engages your focus. And keep doing this until you feel some emotional movement. Until that happens, you really aren't finished with the rejection process.

GET REJECTED!

The only circumstance under which you will not need to master the rejection process is if you are not getting rejected—and if you are not getting rejected you are not doing enough interruptions and initiations with women and you are much less likely to succeed with them.

That's so important we'll say it again: getting rejected is a good sign because it means that you are taking action with women, taking risks and doing what you have to to create abundant relationships with women in your life. Remember our student who said hi to more than 300 women in a week in his ultimately successful quest to get sex and a girl-friend? He says, "I made use of the rejection tools on a daily basis. It kept me alive as I went through lots of women till I found what I was looking for." These tools can help you too.

HOW to Handle Panic and Anxiety Around Women

You need to learn how to handle the inevitable anxiety and fear that comes up when you approach and talk to women. Experiencing fear in these situations is very common, so we're going to teach you some basic skills to overcome panic and anxiety.

Many of us mistakenly think there are men out there who are seduction masters who never experience any fear and can go up to any woman at any time and seduce them. The truth is that we all get scared and fear-ful when approaching women. We often get scared when approaching women for the first time, and so do all of our students. The point is to learn how to handle anxiety and panic and approach women even when you feel nervous.

Many top athletes experience fear and nervousness before going into a big game, but they've learned to use fear to their advantage. They've learned to use the fear as a motivator, as something that helps them get in the flow, rather than something that takes them out of the game. We've heard rumors that hockey god Gordie Howe would puke in the locker room before every game. He would be overcome with anxiety, but he learned how to feel the fear and go for it anyway. Our hope is that you too can learn how to transform your fear and use it to your advantage.

Let's get real: if there's one thing that generates panic, it's going up to women and talking to them. One of the hardest things to do is to initiate interaction with a woman in a place like a bar or the street when you don't have any excuse to talk to her.

Fear hits each man differently. Fear occurs on a spectrum, from anticipatory fear like butterflies in your stomach and slight nervousness to all-out panic and total terror. We've worked with men on all points of the spectrum. The tools in this section are for men who have mild or small amounts of panic. If you suffer from all-out panic attacks with women, you need to look deeper, perhaps to anti-anxiety medication or therapy. We are not therapists or doctors, and handling panic is not our area of expertise. We can tell you that if you have panic attacks there is help. We've had many students overcome extreme anxiety with women by combining therapy, medication and our materials.

Here are a few tools for you to learn and practice. The more you can practice them when you're alone in a woman-free environment, the easier it will be to use them when you're about to approach a woman.

Breathing. Men are often tense around women and forget to breathe, or when they do breathe they take shallow breaths. Practice breathing deeply. Deep breathing is the fundamental skill in overcoming panic because when a person gets tense the first thing that changes is his breathing. It becomes shallow and increases in speed, and all of a sudden his body shifts into fight-or-flight mode. When you breathe rapidly and shallowly, your brain is also affected; you think less clearly and enter a spiral that leads to more panic. The trick is to start deep breathing before you get nervous around women and to continue deep breathing when you approach women.

Here's how you do it: practice breathing slowly and fully into your abdomen. We recommend you breathe in and count to four and then breathe out while counting to four. After a few minutes of breathing deeply, you should be much calmer. Practice this on a daily basis so that you can slow down your breath at will.

Visualizing. Start by closing your eyes and breathe deeply for five or 10 seconds. Next, imagine a relaxing scene. Maybe you imagine you're in bed or on the beach; maybe it's your boyhood home or your favorite nature spot—it doesn't really matter. All that matters is that it anchors a feeling of calm, safety and relaxation. It sounds silly, we realize, but it actually works.

Visualizing a calm scene just before you go up and talk to a woman is very useful in getting yourself into a relaxed, playful mode. The cool part is that you can use the same relaxing scene over and over again, which will help you stay calm. You can keep recalling that scene each time you feel nervous.

Recalling a time you felt powerful and confident. This will affect your posture and breathing, and your overall sense of confidence with women. Start by recalling a time when you really had balls, when you fearlessly went for something and produced an extraordinary result.

When you recall a time you felt powerful, you don't have to draw on a situation where you felt powerful with women. It could be a football game, a race you won, when you asked for a raise, a great speech you gave or any moment of victory in your life. It's a way to boost your confidence. It's a way for you to tell yourself, "Yes, I've got balls, I've done stuff that is amazing, I can do this—no question about it, no doubt." We've all had moments where we've performed beyond what we thought our capabilities were. And you, yes, you, have had those moments too.

If you take a few seconds to recall a time you were powerful, you'll feel a lot more powerful when you approach a woman. Remember those moments and use your past success to fuel your confidence with women today.

Stretching. When you feel stressed and tense, your body in turn tenses up. After you have done some deep breathing and visualized success, it's also useful to stretch your body to help it relax. Stand up and take a few minutes to stretch your body from head to toe. Breathe as you do it. The next time you're stressed and want to approach a woman, go into a corner or go outside and stretch for a few minutes.

Changing your thoughts. If you are like most guys, the moment before you are going to talk to a woman your thoughts get ugly—real ugly. You think about all your past failures, all the ways in which you suck, all the reasons you're a failure with women. In the face of all that self-flagellation, who can be successful? Train yourself to think about something pleasant, even fun, when you're around women. Think about food, sports, sex, your favorite movie, whatever. When you feel stressed and nervous, thinking about something you enjoy will help perk you up so you can have fun.

Not taking your thoughts so seriously. We all think crazy stuff sometimes. But just because you have a thought one moment doesn't mean you are going to have it the next. We hear that people who meditate for years and years often comment that they get to a place where they stop taking their thoughts, feelings and body sensations seriously. They realize that at every moment there are new thoughts and sensations passing through their body, and that's just life.

The experience of meditators suggests that we are always in a state of flux. One moment we might be feeling extreme fear and the next moment the fear will turn into something different. You are always changing, so one way to be relaxed is to think, "I'm not going to have this panic thought for more than a minute or two; then it will change. Remind yourself that your thoughts and body sensations are not real and don't need to dictate your behavior.

Visualizing someone you trust. You may find it calming to picture someone you trust and imagine them offering you support and encouragement. Think of Ron Louis and David Copeland. We are on your team. We are here to encourage you.

Visualize anybody who has been a supportive figure in your life. Who are the supportive figures in your life now? Who are your best friends? Imagine they are there behind you, on your team, encouraging you to go up and talk to that woman you're scared to talk to.

You can even imagine that someone like John Travolta (in his role in the movie *Get Shorty*), a rock star, someone you admire or a political figure is supporting you. Just imagine they are there behind you saying, "Come on, you can do it, you can do it. We have total faith in you!" This technique works very well in building up your confidence.

Taking a walk. Leave wherever you are and walk around the block for a few minutes. While you're out, do some deep breathing and enjoy the fresh air. And while you're walking, think about someone you enjoy being around or an experience that is pleasant. You may want to walk very briskly to change your internal state and get your blood pumping. Taking a walk can be really useful in changing your internal state, clearing your head and calming you down enough to approach the woman you really want to approach

We also recommend that you get aerobic exercise at least three times a week. Men who tend to have panic and anxiety can greatly decrease their stress level by regularly getting moderate amounts of aerobic exercise.

Learning tai chi or yoga. Learning some tai chi, chi kung or yoga postures can help you remain calm. Many students have reported that learning tai chi or yoga is greatly useful in learning to stay calm. You can pick up books on these types of exercise or take courses. Since tai chi, chi kung and yoga tend to be meditative, students often find they can use the skills to stay calm in their daily lives, particularly in stressful situations.

Drinking heavily. Just kidding. You can try this method, but it will usually backfire. Perhaps you'll calm down, but you might also become a belligerent jerk. You need to gauge how often and how much you drink so that you can feel confident and articulate and think clearly when you're around women.

There are a lot of other things that you can do to relax. These are just a few that should be helpful. If there are practices you use to decrease your anxiety, keep doing them. If you hear of other exercises, definitely try them. The point is to find practices you can take on to remain calm and relaxed when you talk to women.

Feeling tense and afraid is perfectly normal, but having tools to overcome your fear is what's most important. Practice a few of these moves before approaching women and your confidence will greatly improve.

Panic and anxiety is something that can be controlled. If you suffer from this problem, no matter where you are on the panic spectrum, there is hope. •

CHAPTER 5
FLIRTING, "WHAT'S THE STORY BEHIND THAT?"

As we've said before, there is a step-by-step sequence of events in seducing a woman. As you learn the skills for flirting and talking to women and practice them with women, you'll probably find it helpful to remember the phases of seducing a woman.

The first phase of seducing a woman is getting yourself ready. You always need to be getting your mind clear and determining if anything is stopping you. If there's a past rejection stopping you, you must get over it (see the previous two chapters). You must get your mind clear; remember and celebrate your past victories and get yourself into a peak performance state. You must be ready for possible rejection, and have handled your panic. Whether you're on a coffee date, about to say hi to a woman or going for a first kiss, you are always going to be battling yourself and your own frame of mind. That's phase one.

The second phase of seducing a woman is interrupting her and getting her attention. You must initiate with women, and it takes guts to do that. It takes guts to initiate the first kiss. It takes guts to initiate getting her phone number and email address. It takes guts to initiate everything. And that's your job. Never fail to remember that it's your job, exclusively.

The third phase is the rapport phase, the romance-building phase. That is when you are having a connection with somebody in which she feels like you understand her, she feels like she understands you and you just have a nice conversational flow. The skills in this book will help you accomplish this.

The fourth phase introduces a physical connection. She sees you as a potential romantic partner. This involves light sensuality.

Finally, the fifth phase is getting into more "heavy" sexual stuff. You started by getting yourself ready, interrupting her, developing rapport and making her see you as a romantic possibility. Now you are initiating that next foray into sexual contact.

Although this book focuses on talking to women, for more information on dating you can read *How to Succeed with Women* and visit our web site at www.howtosucceedwithwomen.com.

During a typical interaction with a woman, you are going to go through stages one through five over and over again. You are always going to come back to your state of mind and getting yourself prepped. You are always interrupting her on a deeper and deeper level.

But these phases can also happen out of sequence. You are constantly going in as deep as you can go and then backpedaling. You go in and you are holding hands and you stop holding hands then you go back into the interruption phase. You might be making out and all of a sudden find yourself back in the rapport-building phase. A date is unpredictable. You have to let that flow happen.

Before we get into the specific talking and flirting skills, there are a few general concepts we should cover: the three time frames of an interaction with a woman, leaving her wanting more and other factors in how you appear to a woman.

The Three Time Frames of Interaction with Women

If you are going to succeed in talking to a woman, you need to know just how urgent the situation with her is. Every man has had a wonderful woman walk out of his life forever because he wasn't conscious of how urgent it was to take a risk with her right then. Understanding the three time frames of an interaction will help keep that from happening.

You only have a few minutes. In this situation you only have a few minutes, or maybe just a few seconds, to make contact. You are on a train or in a line and this is your one-and-only chance. You say hi to her and it leads to a conversation. You have to get her number or email address right then. If you blow it, she is going to be gone—literally. In this situation you have to cut to the chase quickly. You have to risk a lot to get her phone number or email address or it's all over.

One of our students told us about being in one of these situations recently while in line at the post office. There was a pretty girl who was also in line who made eye contact with him several times. He said hi and they started to chat, but her turn came up at the counter and she was drawn away.

After she finished her business and was leaving, he got out of line and followed her into the lobby. "Excuse me," he said, "but I just got the strong feeling that I ought to say hi to you. I know it seems strange, but I just had this feeling about you. Could I have your email address, and perhaps we could get together sometime?" He had a brief window of opportunity and he needed to take a big risk, so he took it. If he hadn't, she would have been out of his life forever.

You have a few hours. This is a situation like an all-day seminar, a party or a work-related activity where you know the woman you are interested in is going to be around for a little while. You don't have to risk it all right away; you can afford to wait, to take small risks with her over a few hours rather than taking a really big risk all at once.

You have days, weeks or longer. This is the waitress you can go back and see over and over or the woman in your aerobics class who always works out at 5 p.m. on Tuesdays and Thursdays. You can risk much more slowly with these women and build a connection over time.

Knowing these three time frames helps you know how much you must risk and how quickly you must do so. If you are putting gasoline into your car and the woman at the next car is attractive and you want to talk to her then you had better risk a lot right then, because she is about to disappear from your life. On the other hand, if that same woman shows up at an eight-week class you are taking, you don't have to risk big right away by going for her phone number or email address. You can risk big if you want, but you can also take smaller risks and seduce her over time.

You can also look at this as a risk spectrum. For instance, you have to take more risk when you ask for the number of a woman you are in line with than you do to get her number when you see a woman twice a week in your aerobics class.

Leave Her Wanting More

It's best to leave a woman wanting more. That means it's better if your conversations with her are short.

That's not how most guys flirt with women. With most guys, if an interaction with a woman is going well, they push it and keep talking until something bad happens. Only when there's a problem or bad feeling with the woman do they stop. That means they always manage to end their interactions with women on sour notes. That's bad.

These guys think, "Wow, this is going great. Therefore, I'm not going to try to get her number and close the deal, I'm just going to keep talking." Or they think, "Wow, this is going great. Therefore, I'm not going to come back and talk to her more later; I'm going to stay here and be amazed that it's going well until she inevitably gets bored. When she gets bored I will get tense and then when I get tense I will mess everything up and she will finally say, 'Oh, I have to leave.'"

Okay, maybe no guy actually thinks that—but that's how it works out in practice.

Unfortunately, you will find a way to blow it during those first interactions if you give it enough time. Therefore you have to leave while things are going well, and leave her wanting more.

Your flirting interactions need to be long enough to give her a pleasurable experience and leave her wanting to see you again. If it's going well, don't break the rules—get out of there on a high note so she's left wanting more of you, not tired of you and wanting less.

That is also a way to keep yourself empowered. If you stop your flirting interactions with women while they are still fun, you can be happy about how well it went. It'll charge you up. And that will keep your ability to seduce alive.

InfLUEnCInG HOW YOU APPear to women

As you start using the techniques in this book, you'll naturally begin to find yourself in conversations with women. Let's go over a few pointers about sounding and looking good.

Breathe more deeply. As we mentioned before, many men breathe into and speak from their upper chests and throats. This gives their voices a nasal sound and it makes them sound tense when they talk to women.

Practice breathing from deeper in your body. Breathe more deeply and let your stomach go in and out as you do. Then take a deep breath so you can feel your voice originating from deeper in your body rather than exclusively from your throat and head. This will give your voice more resonance and make it far more attractive to listen to.

Adjust your tempo. Over the next day or so, let yourself become aware of the speed at which you talk. Some men talk so quickly that they're exhausting for women to listen to. If you tend to "speed rap" people, you need to practice slowing down. If you notice yourself talking really quickly, pause and take a deep breath. Sometimes blinking slowly helps.

By the same token, we've worked with some men who talk so slowly and ponderously that it's hypnotic—and exceptionally boring—to listen to them. If you're a man who talks very slowly, you might consider being a little more animated in your speaking. Breathing more deeply will help with this, as will allowing yourself to express more of your excitement when you are talking to people. Practice sounding more excited when you talk with people and see how it feels.

Make eye contact. If you are looking all over the place or staring at the floor, you are going to be unattractive to women. While your interaction with a woman should not be a staring contest, do maintain some eye contact with her.

THE FIVE FLIRTING SKILLS

Now that you have some facility with interrupting women and saying hi and we've gone over some other fundamentals, we can start teaching you the specific flirting skills.

There are two great things about these flirting skills. First, they fit together really well. Once you understand and start to use these skills, you'll see how you can flow from one to another and really have a romantic, fun, flirtatious, genuine, nonmanipulative interaction with a woman.

Second, these skills are eminently learnable. You can learn the basics quickly, practice them, review your progress and get good at them. They aren't magic; you don't have to be supercharismatic man or a naturally gifted hypnotist to use them. These skills, along with the skills for interrupting and initiating with women, will help you create romantic connections with women.

There are five flirting skills that you will learn from this book:

- Asking "What's the story behind that?"
- The Goodbye Introduction
- Situational Flirting
- Deepening
- Romantic Questions and Romantic Conversations

We'll deal with the first flirting skill right now and cover the others in later chapters.

ASKING "WHAT'S THE STORY BEHIND THAT?"

"What's the story behind that?" is about noticing the details of a woman's appearance and making those details topics of conversation.

This is easy to do if you understand women's relationship to details. The world of women is in the details. She works hard on the details of her appearance. Noticing those details and complimenting her on them is extremely seductive, and it's something you can easily learn to do in your conversations with her.

Noticing and acknowledging details about a woman separates you from other men. Most men don't see details, or if they do, they don't comment on them. Noticing details sets you apart from the crowd. It makes you more attractive.

"What's the story behind that?" is a simple question to ask after you've said hi and noticed some detail of a woman's presentation. If you've gotten at all good at saying hi, using this skill is easy. "What's the story behind that?" is an excellent question to ask a woman: it's open-ended and it gives her a chance to talk about something that might be important to her.

If a woman is wearing an interesting-looking ring or earrings or if she has an interesting briefcase or pin—basically, if there's anything about her to which she may have paid special attention—you can say, "Oh, that's a very interesting pin" (or whatever). "I don't see pins like that every day. What's the story behind that?"

Almost every woman has a detail about her about which you could ask "What's the story behind that?" You might say, "That looks like an interesting book you're reading. What's the story behind that?" or "I see you're carrying *Utne Reader* magazine. That looks interesting—what's the story behind that?" or "I haven't seen a laptop computer like that before. What's the story behind that?" It is a great way to open up almost any conversation.

We can hear you saying, "But asking 'What's the story behind that magazine you are reading' doesn't make sense!" You're right—and that lack of "sense" is part of the power of the question. It's very open, so she's free to interpret it any way she wants, and that might lead to something interesting. At the worst, she'll ask you, "What do you mean?" and you can ask a follow-up question such as "What is it about that magazine that you like?" or "Are there any articles in it that particularly interested you?"

Of course, it's better to notice details about physical appearance that are more meaningful to her than her laptop or the magazine she is carrying, but there may not always be something like that available. If so, it's fine to go for something mundane.

RON: Asking "What's the story behind that?" can work really well. For instance, I was talking to this woman in line at a coffee shop. She was right in front of me, so I said hi and she said hi back. I noticed she had on this Indian bracelet with all these markings on it, so I said to her, "Wow, that is a really interesting bracelet that you have on. I haven't seen anything like that before. What's the story behind that?" She said, "Oh, I got this on my trip to India." I followed up: "Oh wow, a trip to India? That's really interesting. Are you someone who likes to travel?" She said, "Yeah, it was an amazing experience," and we easily got into a conversation about traveling and her trip to India.

We'll show you more detailed examples of how to sustain and deepen the conversations that "What's the story behind that?" will start. For now, all you have to worry about is saying hi, noticing a detail and getting one simple question out of your mouth: "What's the story behind that?"

Screwing Up "What's the Story Behind That?"

You can screw up any flirting skill, and "What's the story behind that?" is no different.

As we mentioned before, "What's the story behind that?" is a very open-ended question. That means it doesn't limit her answer. If you ask, "What's the story behind that necklace?" she can answer by talking about how she got it in India or how she made it herself or how it always reminds her of her first dog or whatever she wants. The question doesn't limit the range of her answer, which is good.

But if you ask the question incorrectly, you will limit her possible answers, which is bad. See if you can spot the errors in the following two examples.

We once had a coaching client who reported to us that he used "What's the story behind that?" and it totally didn't work. We asked him to tell us what happened. He said, "Okay, I was in the elevator at work with this woman and I saw that she had on a really interesting pin, so I said to her, 'Oh, that's an interesting pin. Where did you get it?' And she said, 'Oh, I got it at a store.' That was the end of the conversation—it didn't go anywhere at all."

Another coaching client saw a woman who was wearing a really interesting scarf. He said to her, "Wow, that's a really interesting scarf you're wearing. Is that a family heirloom?" She gasped and said, "Oh god, I hope not—I hate my family." End of conversation. He didn't get her number, or anything else from her.

Did you spot the errors? Both of these men asked the question in ways that limited the answers the women could give. The first guy said, "That's an interesting pin. Where did you get it?" Well, there's a very simple answer to that question: "I got it at a store." The question limited the kind of answer she can give; she could only talk about where she obtained it, which was probably boring for both her and the man.

On the other hand, saying, "That's an interesting pin, what's the story behind that?" is very open. She can answer with almost anything that interests her. She could say, "I got it in New Zealand" or "I got it at the mall" or "I got it for myself with my Christmas money." It leaves her with an incredibly wide range of possible answers, which makes it easier for you to ask follow-up questions: "Do you like to travel?" or "What about it made you buy it?"

In the second example, the man said, "That's a really interesting scarf you're wearing. Is that a family heirloom?" Once again, he limited her possible answers, and in this case, he forced a conversational direction that was upsetting to her. If he had asked, "What's the story behind that?" she could have talked about what she wanted to talk about and things would have worked out much better.

There's a great sequence starting to build here. Hi can lead very naturally to "What's the story behind that?" and that leads into the other flirting skills.

CONCLUSION

"What's the story behind that?" is an immensely powerful flirting question. It gets most women to open up immediately and tell you intimate details about themselves. After they've told you these details, it's harder for them to think of you as a jerk; after all, if you were a jerk, why would they open up so much to you?

When you're talking to a woman, be it a salesgirl behind a counter or a woman at a party, check to see if she's wearing anything that looks unusual or personal. It might be a pin, a necklace, a piece of clothing or a bracelet. When you see it, ask her, "What's the story behind that?" It's a powerful conversation starter. •

How to Talk to Women

CHaPTer 6
ROManTiC MOVeS, GOODBYe
inTRODUCTiOn

THe Seven ROManTiC MOVeS

We're about to teach you seven Romantic Moves (also called Flirting Moves) to memorize and implement in your life. When you implement these moves while talking to women your success rate will increase greatly. If you conduct Romantic Conversations and don't integrate these moves, you'll likely stay stuck in the dreaded friend zone. So it's time to get seductive and learn the Romantic Moves.

The main reason some men get stuck in the friend zone is because they don't know how to show their romantic interest. Other men get stuck in the friend zone because they're afraid of being rejected. Men in both categories can learn the Romantic Moves, use them without risking their hearts and souls, and finally stop coming across as perpetual friends.

If you're like a lot of our students, you've looked at the bad boys who get women and decided you weren't going be like them. You probably decided that if getting women meant you'd have to lie, manipulate women or act like a jerk, you would just give up dating.

There is good news, however: you don't need to be a jerk to get women, though you can learn some things from the bad boys. The bad boys are willing to show their romantic interest right away and risk rejection. The bad boys are willing to be upfront with their sexual interest. You can learn to be up front and show your romantic interest to women in ways that allow them to feel appreciated and respected. We'll show you how.

When you meet a woman for the first time, it's crucial that she knows you're a romantic possibility. If she sees you as only a friend, it's hard to become her lover. We believe that women decide within three minutes of meeting a man if he's a potential lover or not. If you send clear signals that you're only interested in being friends (by not doing the Romantic Moves), you'll blow your chances of something more intimate developing later.

Men often think that the Romantic Moves do not apply if a woman is extremely attractive. You follow the same rules when dealing with hot women as you do with others. Show your romantic interest right away with all women.

It's important for you to familiarize yourself with all of the Romantic Moves. Find the ones that are toughest for you and keep practicing them until they feel natural. Hopefully some of them will be easy for you. If so, keep practicing them and refining your skills. After a while, when you're familiar with all seven moves, you'll find yourself effortlessly integrating them into your flirting and your conversations with women.

Romantic Moves

You must learn all seven of the moves and practice them. When unsuccessful seducers find that a few Romantic Moves are difficult or scary, they give up. Grapple with yourself and overcome any resistance you have to practicing and integrating the Romantic Moves into your dating life.

Another pitfall to which unsuccessful seducers succumb is only using one or two Romantic Moves. If you only use one or two moves when you flirt with women you will not be successful. You will not send enough clear, strong signals about your interest. When you meet a woman for the first time, you need to do at least four of the Romantic Moves so you send a clear signal that you are romantically interested.

Look into her eyes "too long." Looking into a woman's eyes "too long" creates a moment of intimacy between you and her. In holding eye contact, you're creating a little moment in which she recognizes that you're romantically interested in her. A friend would avoid eye contact and be more cautious, but you're no longer just a friend. You are stepping into the potential lover category and creating moments of intimacy by making eye contact with her.

Here's how to do it: At some point while you're speaking, or during a conversational lull, hold eye contact for just a beat too long, just until it's a little uncomfortable.

It's important to remember that this is not a staring contest, just a little moment of intimacy. When Bob the bad seducer looks at a woman, he stares too long and too deeply. He tenses up his body, leans in close to her face and stares at her long and hard. The key to looking into a woman's eyes "too long" is to avoid turning it into a big deal. Look into her eyes for a beat too long—just long enough to create a special moment.

If you're a guy who tends to avoid eye contact and stare at the floor, you need to practice looking into women's eyes when you talk. Having a difficult time making and holding eye contact is a very common problem, but there is help. The cure is to start looking women directly in the eye for a few seconds and then walking away.

You can develop new skills with women, like talking and maintaining eye contact, by training your nervous system in small doses to do uncomfortable things and experiment with new behaviors. When you practice stretching yourself in new ways, you will eventually become desensitized and feel comfortable being with women. If you're willing to start small and build your confidence slowly over time, you'll eventually overcome your fears and be successful. If you have a hard time looking a woman in the eyes when you talk, start practicing today. Over the next few months you will feel more confident and comfortable initiating and holding eye contact.

Let's go over how to look into a woman's eyes "too long" once again. Look into her eyes and hold eye contact just a wee bit too long so you get into the intimacy zone. Practice holding eye contact and practice getting caught looking. Looking into a woman's eyes too long will greatly enhance your seductive presence.

Make decisions quickly and easily. Men who are decisive come across as confident, strong, powerful. Indecisive men come across as scared, intimidated, afraid to be themselves. How do you want to come across to women?

When you're with a woman, make decisions quickly and easily. If you're on a date and you can sit in one corner of the coffee shop or the other, choose quickly. If you're ordering wine at a bar, decide quickly. If you're selecting a movie to watch, do so quickly. If you're picking a place to meet for a date, pick quickly. When you're out with a woman, she needs to see that you're a decisive man. This doesn't mean you turn into a decision Nazi and never ask for her input. It does mean, however, that when there are times for quick decisions during a date you act decisively.

Wink. Winking is a lost art. Most men don't wink at women. Why are we recommending it? Because winking at women is seductive, simple, fun and intimate. Friends don't wink at each other; potential lovers do.

Here's how to do it:

• Lower one eyelid and then lift it back up.

It just takes a second and is very easy. It helps to smile after you wink to make the interaction feel warmer. You can wink at any point in a conversation with a woman. Maybe you're talking to her and you're both laughing about something and you give her a little wink. Maybe you're looking at a woman across a room and you give her a wink. Winking creates a little intimate moment between you and her. The key to success in winking at a woman is to be subtle and make sure the wink is a quick shared moment between the two of you, not a long uncomfortable ordeal.

Here's how to blow it:

- If you contort your face and look like an axe murderer while blinking both of your eyes at rapid speed, you will not come across as romantic.
- If you wink at a woman and then run toward her, you will look like a stalker.
- If you wink at a woman and then stick out your tongue in an overtly sexual manner, you will come across as a jerk.
- If you wink at a woman and then stare deeply into her eyes, you will look like a scary guy.
- If you wink at a woman and look terrified instead of confident, you will come across as a scared, immature boy.

We hope you get the point.

Winking is a great romantic move because it's not something most men do; it's out of the ordinary. When you wink at a woman it catches her attention and draws her in.

Check out her body. Checking out a woman's body does not mean you stare at her cleavage for hours and hours (even though we all love to see great cleavage). This does not mean you drop some change on the ground and try to look up her skirt while you're picking up the coins that fell in front of her. This means you check out her body in a respectful way.

There's a paradox about many women. On the one hand, they're offended when you stare and check out their bodies too long. On the other hand, they work out all the time so they can have great bodies, dress great and wear push-up bras. Women want you to look at their bodies so they feel appreciated; they just want you to be somewhat subtle so they don't feel completely objectified. Yes, it's a rough line to walk sometimes, but we've got some tips that'll be useful in figuring out this mess.

Here's how to do it:

- Start by looking in her eyes.
- In less than a second, move your eyes from hers and then sweep down her body.
- Come back up to her eyes and face, smile and keep on talking like nothing happened.

With this method a woman will see you looking at her body, but because it's so fast and starts and ends with her face it comes across as respectful.

Checking out a woman's body is a good move because it's not something a friend would do. A friend might wait until she wasn't looking and then try to look down her shirt. When you're able to check out a woman quickly, you're letting her know you're romantically interested in her and not a jerk.

Here's how to blow it:

- Get lost in staring at her breasts.
- Stare at her crotch and lick your lips.
- Nod your head emphatically up and down.
- Say "I am staring at your bodacious tits" when she asks you what you're looking at.
- Tense up your face and show her the whites of your eyes until you look like you're going into a grand-mal seizure.

Train yourself to be able to check out a woman in less than a second. You're checking out women all the time anyway, so you might as well start practicing this method.

Keep your body powerful. Who are some of your seduction heroes in the movies? Is it Will Smith? John Travolta? Billy Bob Thornton? Clint Eastwood? Humphrey Bogart? The name of your screen hero isn't important; the point is that you'll likely be more seductive if you model your behavior and posture on your hero. Men who are seductive hold their body in a powerful way so when they're standing, sitting or moving they come across as both fascinated and fascinating. The way to do this is to pretend that you are fascinated, fascinating and powerful and then stand and move in that way.

Let's do an experiment. Right now, as you read this book, sit in your chair like you're bored to tears. Now sit up and read this book like you're getting a million dollars of value from Louis & Copeland. What's the difference in your body posture? What's the difference in your attention? How does your body feel? When you are in a state where you are attentive and keeping your body powerful it will show in your body language and in your presentation.

When you're interacting with a woman and keeping your body powerful, you're not distracted. You're paying attention to her, not checking out other women. You're not looking at your watch, reading a newspaper, messing around with your palmtop computer—you're only focused on her. We're not suggesting you have a wild, maniacal look in your eye; don't stare at her cross-eyed and never blink while talking. Just focus on the woman you're talking to and keep your body powerful.

Compliment her. When you compliment a woman the way a friend compliments a woman, you say, "Wow, that's a really nice briefcase you have." When you compliment a woman the way a potential lover compliments a woman, you say, "Wow, you are a beautiful woman. You have really beautiful eyes. It's really a pleasure to meet you." In complimenting a woman the way a lover does, you stay away from impersonal compliments. As a potential lover, you want to let her know that you're noticing romantic details about her and you're willing to take risks in talking to her.

When you compliment women you can say things like "I just got lost in how beautiful you are for a second" or "You have an amazing sense of style" or "Your smile brightens up the whole room." If you're being introduced to a woman by a mutual friend, for instance, you might say, "Oh, so this is the beautiful Jennifer I've heard so much about."

When complimenting a woman, be on the lookout for details. When you can see and acknowledge the details that a woman has put a lot of effort into, you come across as a potential lover. As we said, a friend compliments a woman on her briefcase, car or something impersonal. A potential lover compliments a woman on her earrings, necklace, hair, smile or something more intimate.

Sometimes friends and lovers may notice the same thing about a woman but they will bring it up in very different ways. A friend might notice a necklace and say, "That's a very nice necklace." A potential lover might say, "Wow, that's a really lovely necklace you're wearing, and it just makes you glow even more." A friend might say, "I like how your belt matches your shoes." A potential lover would say, "I noticed your belt and shoes match. They draw out the color in your eyes and make you look even more beautiful."

You'll make mistakes along they way—we all do. One of the situations many of our students need to encounter is offending a woman by pushing a compliment too far. That can be a good thing to experience. Flirting with women requires risk, and when you risk with a woman, sometimes you will accidentally offend her. This is part of life. The only way to stay perfectly safe is to remain in the friend zone. If you're willing to take some risks and give a woman some compliments, you'll find out how to push the boundary between friend and lover, despite the occasional mistake.

As you practice complimenting women, it's important to find your own unique compliment style. Do you feel comfortable complimenting a woman on her smile? What feels too overtly sexual to you? What seems cheesy to you? Get out there and find the style that's best for you. When you do, your confidence and success will increase tremendously.

Whisper to her. When you whisper to a woman, you create a moment of intimacy between the two of you. It's like the rest of the world is shut out for a second and you're alone together.

If you have the opportunity to whisper during a conversation, it's a great move to make. For example, you might whisper to a woman, "I have to confess that you're really beautiful," or "I really am enjoying talking to you."

Whispering is a good tool to use to emphasize romantic talk.

Here's how to do it:

• Lean into her and say a few quiet words; then lean out and talk normally.

Whispering's a way of drawing in your personal space and making the conversation more intimate.

Here's how to blow it:

- Pretend you're mute or you've had a tracheotomy.
- Whisper like you're speaking some incomprehensible foreign language.
- Whisper dozens of times during a date. Once or twice is quite enough!

These are fundamental moves to make when you're with women to insure that you won't come across as a friend. When you use the Romantic Moves, you'll turn any conversation into a romantic one and show a woman you're romantically interested. If you hold eye contact "too long," make decisions quickly and easily, wink at a woman, check out her body, compliment her, keep your body powerful and whisper to her, you will become a seduction machine.

Keep track of how many Romantic Moves you do in your daily life. Which are easy and which are difficult? Find the moves that scare you most and try them anyway. The more you practice them, the less intimidating they'll be. If one of the Romantic Moves is easy for you, refine it by practicing it often. We want you to feel comfortable with these moves while pushing yourself to go outside of your normal comfort zone. These moves are going to bring out the romantic you.

THE GOODBYE INTRODUCTION

The Goodbye Introduction is another way of initiating with a woman, showing your romantic interest and complimenting her on a deep level. It's risky in that you are going out of your way and showing romantic interest directly. At the same time, it's low-risk in that it addresses her fears, so is not threatening to her. It's also quick and it gives you an easy exit if the interaction doesn't go the way you'd hoped.

WHEN TO USE THE GOODBYE INTRODUCTION

When you haven't had a chance to say hi. The Goodbye Introduction is a great thing to use with women you haven't had a chance to say hi to. She may be across the bar or working out at your gym or a waitress who didn't serve your table or any woman you see and want to approach, but the natural flow of things hasn't thrown the two of you together.

When you are leaving anyway. The Goodbye Introduction is a great last thing to do in many social situations. The Goodbye Introduction can be a fun, exciting way to connect with a hot woman when you're leaving a bar, restaurant, store or wherever you may be.

When you want to interact with a woman who intimidates you. The Goodbye Introduction is designed to be over quickly; it doesn't put you in a situation where you are faced with a woman without having any idea what to say or do. It's simple, easy, to the point and fast.

When you want to build your self-esteem with women.
When you're feeling too intimidated to try to have a long conversation
with a hot woman, the Goodbye Introduction might be exactly what you
need. It's not designed to get you her number or email address, though
you can use it for that; it's designed to get you into the game of seduction on a much deeper level than simply saying hi.

How the Goodbye Introduction Works

Imagine you're at the gym and you see a woman who's really attractive.
But she's busy lifting weights, and it seems like your gym isn't such a
friendly place anyway.

Here's what you do: leave the gym when she is between sets or stretching. Then, on your way out, introduce yourself like this (smile while you
do it!): "Hi, I'm just leaving and I only have a second here, but before I
go I really wanted to introduce myself to the woman who has such wonderful form. My name is Ron." She'll say something back like "Oh hi,
my name is Mandy." Then you say, "I've gotta go, but I hope to see you
here again." Then you leave.

This simple interaction creates an opening for you to talk to her next time
you see her ("Hi Mandy, how are you?"). It also gives you a way of interacting with her for the first time without there being much risk for either of
you. Because you tell her right away that you are leaving, she's less likely
to be afraid of you wasting lots of her time. It also builds your esteem and
teaches your nervous system that you can actually survive talking to beautiful women, which makes it more likely that you'll do it again in the future.

The Parts of the Goodbye Introduction

The Goodbye Introduction has four parts, and they're all important:

Tell her you're leaving. You tell her you are leaving by saying something like "I have to go now" or "I've gotta run, my friends are waiting for me outside."

This is a very important step. Most of the time, women you don't know well are going to ask themselves some combination of three things when you first interrupt them or take a conversation into deeper, riskier territory. These questions are about her safety; they are "What is he going to do to me?," "How long will it take?" and "Why is he saying this to me?"

This is why, when you do the Goodbye Introduction, your first words are "I have to leave." Saying that you have to leave makes it easier for her to listen to you because it answers two of her most pressing questions. She knows the interaction won't take long, and since it won't take long, there's less bad stuff that you'll have time to do to her. Addressing those safety questions is important, and saying "I have to leave" or some variation thereof handles that nicely.

It's important to know that you can't just answer her safety questions explicitly through some sort of direct, dignified conversation, which men sometimes try to do. Men who try to allay women's fears directly almost always fail; they end up saying something like "I'm not a stalker or anything, I wanted to meet you" or "Don't be afraid, I just wanted to say hi."

These never work, because saying these things is so incredibly suspicious that they steer a woman back into her safety questions. She'll instantly ask herself, "Why is he telling me he's not a stalker? Is it because he is one? What's he going to do to me? How long will it take?" She ends up terrified, and the conversation goes nowhere good.

Saying "I have to go," on the other hand, isn't at all suspicious and answers her safety questions well enough for her to relax at least a little. This allows her to be more open and receptive to what you say next, when you…

Tell her you couldn't leave without complimenting her. You simply say, "but I just couldn't leave without introducing myself to the woman who…"

Compliment her. The compliment itself will depend on the situation you are in. What is it about her that you're admiring? Are you admiring her style? her posture? her radiance? her smile? Whatever it is, you compliment it. (This is within reason, of course—if you're admiring a woman's breasts, for instance, we shouldn't have to tell you that saying "I couldn't leave without introducing myself to the woman who's got one hell of a rack" is not going to sound very seductive.) Find something to admire about her that she'll see as a compliment and give it to her—say something like "the woman who is so incredibly radiant" or "who has such a beautiful smile."

Introduce yourself. This part is simple—simply state your name.

She'll probably respond by telling you her name and being friendly. After all, what does she have to lose if you're about to leave anyway? From there you can either make some chitchat (which we'll talk about soon) or leave, your self-esteem increased by having taken a risk and having had a real, romantic interaction with an attractive woman.

The Goodbye Introduction doesn't usually get you a date right away. What it does do is make you into the kind of guy who approaches women directly and romantically, and a big part of becoming a seducer is becoming that kind of guy. At this point in the seduction skill building, the point is not to get her in bed; the point is to get you to be the kind of guy who can do this sort of thing. The Goodbye Introduction builds that aggressive, seductive muscle, which is what will help you succeed with women.

Furthermore, if you use the Goodbye Introduction at a gym, bar or anyplace you might see the woman again, you now have an opening with her: you've complimented her, you've introduced yourself to her as a powerful man and you know her name. Next time you see her, you can say hi and use your other flirting skills with her.

Using the Goodbye Introduction to Get Contact Information

You can use the Goodbye Introduction to get a woman's phone number or email address. If you say, "I was just leaving and I really gotta go, but I just had to stop and say hello to the woman who is so beautiful. Hi, my name is David." She might say, "Hi, my name is Sarah." From there you can say pretty much anything. If you're at the gym, for instance, you can ask her how she likes the gym or how often she works out. You can ask "What's the story behind that?" or use any of the other flirting skills.

When you are ready, you leave—and we suggest you do this while the conversation is still fun. First, say to her, "You know, I really have to go, but you seem like an interesting person and I would really like to know you a little better. What would it be like if we got together sometime? Can I have your email address or phone number?" If she says yes, great! Take her info and be gone. If she says no, well, you have to leave anyway. Say, "Well, it's been nice to meet you!" and go.

Examples

As you can see, the Goodbye Introduction is really very simple. You approach her, tell her you're leaving, tell her you couldn't leave without complimenting her, compliment her, introduce yourself and either leave or stay and take the conversation farther.

Here are some examples:

- "Hi! I'm just leaving now, but before I went, I had to come up and tell you that you have such a beautiful smile, it lights up the whole room. I just had to let you know that before I left. By the way, my name is Ron."

- "Hi, I have to go—my friends are waiting for me outside—but before I left I had to come up and tell you that you look incredibly beautiful. By the way, my name is Donald."

- "Hi, I've gotta run right now, but before I do I just had to take the risk of coming up and telling you that you have such a beautiful smile. By the way, my name is David."

- "Hi, I'm just on my way out and only have a second, but before I went I just had to come up and tell you that you have an amazing sense of style. I wish I had to time to stay and seduce you, but I really have to go. By the way, my name is Ron."

Common Goodbye Introduction Mistakes

Skipping the first part. The most common error men make with this is skipping the first part of the Goodbye Introduction. They start talking to a woman but they don't tell her "I'm about to leave, so I only have a moment to talk to you." This leaves her not knowing what you are going to do to her or how long it will take and sends her right back into her safety questions. She thinks, "Oh my god, what is he going to do and how long is this going to take?" You've got to tell her you only have a moment and will be leaving, even if the contact stretches out into a much longer conversation.

Not really complimenting her. If you're used to being just friends with women, it can be very hard to compliment them on something romantic or sensual. You might be afraid to let a women know that you think she is beautiful. You might be embarrassed or worry that your compliment might hurt her in some way. You might worry that everyone will know what you said to her and will laugh at you.

When you let these fears run you, you're likely to give a tepid compliment, like "You have a really nice briefcase" or "Those are nice shoes." Such mild compliments don't show your romantic interest and don't show that you're the kind of guy who's willing to take some risk with women. You're likely to come across as too mild, and that's not good.

Not feeling good about doing it. Having said that, if you're very shy, giving a mild compliment ("That's a very nice pin you're wearing") might be all you can do at first. If so, do it and celebrate that you did it; if you're shy, that may be a big step. Don't expect it to blow her away, because it won't. But it may give you the confidence you need to give a bigger compliment next time, and that's all that really matters.

We had one student who would do the Goodbye Introduction and hated every minute of it. If women didn't drop to their knees to give him oral sex right then, he felt like a complete failure. This made him seem grave, heavy and even scary to women, so he never got the result he was looking for. You have to let yourself feel good about what you do. Doing a Goodbye Introduction is a big step, and no matter how it turns out you should feel good about it.

Not practicing out loud. Practice possible Goodbye Introductions out loud. This is crucial. There's a huge difference between reading the examples in this book and actually speaking them out loud. We recommend that you memorize one or two of these and practice them 10 or 20 times out loud. You have to get used to having these words come out of your mouth so that when you're in front of a woman you can just open your mouth and the right words will come out.

Being unwilling to work your way up. You don't need to go for the hottest women in the world and do this seemingly massive thing if it's too terrifying. You may want to practice this at first with a women whom you aren't massively attracted to just to get the experience.

Waiting for it not to feel risky or scary. It's worth knowing that the first few times you do the Goodbye Introduction will be very scary for you. You'll be afraid that something terrible will happen or that she'll be incredibly upset by it or that she'll laugh at you or that everyone will know what you did and you'll be a complete and utter fool in everyone's eyes. After you've done it a few times you'll know that it's really not that big a deal, and it'll get much easier to do. The problem is you have to go through those first few scary times to get to that point. If you wait for it not to feel risky before you try, you'll never try.

Even after you've learned that you can do the Goodbye Introduction without being instantly struck down by lightning, there will still be a scary moment every time you do it, right before you open your mouth to talk. That's the moment of commitment, the moment the sky diver experiences right as he's about to jump out of the airplane. You can't wait for the fear to go away before you do it. You just have to jump. Open your mouth and say the Goodbye Introduction.

CONCLUSION

Many men are afraid to do the Romantic, Flirting Moves, or the Goodbye Introduction. But when we talk to women, they tell us that hearing a Goodbye Introduction or experiencing some Romantic Moves with a man often makes their entire day. It's a nice thing to do. Contrary to what you may believe, you can be a sweet guy and really make a women's day by flirting with her and showing romantic interest. Don't deprive women of this fun, feel-good experience! •

CHaPter 7
situational Flirting

There you are in front of a hot woman and you want to flirt with her. Maybe she's the receptionist at your dentist's office or the waitress at your luncheonette or the woman who at the mall who's selling you a new tie. You need a good way to flirt with women in these and many other normal, day-to-day situations. When you encounter a woman, you need to be able to flirt with her in a fun way that shows her you're a guy who provides laughs and is stimulating to be around. Situational Flirting is the key.

WHat is situational Flirting?

You've probably seen men who were really good at joking around and kidding with women. Perhaps you've even had moments where you were that guy. Men who are good at kidding around with women and who can make that kidding romantic are practicing Situational Flirting.

Situational Flirting involves two key skills: creative misinterpretation and asking outrageous questions. Creative misinterpretation happens when you take some detail in the environment that you and the woman are in and act as though that item is dramatically different than it is. You then ask an outrageous question about that misinterpretation. You will learn how to do this in this chapter.

For instance, you may be interacting with a woman who has a camera. You may make the creative misinterpretation that her camera can steal souls and then ask the outrageous question: "Oh, I see you have a camera—it's not going to steal my soul, is it?"

This joke is an opening for her to joke back with you. Many women will respond humorously, saying something like, "No, this isn't my soul-stealing camera—I left that one at home." At the very least, most women will smile and laugh. As the playful interaction progresses, you can add, "I think your beauty has stolen my soul already." Then you're really in the realm of effective Situational Flirting.

Situational Flirting comes down to finding something in the environment that you can creatively misinterpret and make a joke about or ask an "Outrageous Question" about. If you can do that, you can practice Situational Flirting.

WHY Practice Situational Flirting?

You need to practice Situational Flirting to solve some of the early problems that shows up in any interaction with a woman you've just met: How are you going to make a light, enjoyable connection? How are you going to build that initial state of rapport? And how are you going to do it in a way that is fun and enjoyable for both of you?

Look at it from her point of view: she's worried that you're a creep. You need to create an enjoyable, memorable experience together that shows her you're a trustworthy, fun guy who she might want to spend time with.

Situational Flirting works well on all these problems. It's fun, light, pleasant, enjoyable and energizing for you both. It creates a shared reality between you, a fantasy world that the two of you can revisit on future occasions (more on this later). And it makes her look forward to seeing you again.

THE SEVEN KEYS OF SITUATIONAL FLIRTING

Remember that dating is a numbers game. As you begin to practice Situational Flirting, it's a good idea to remember our old adage: "Dating is a numbers game." Situational Flirting is not going to work 100 percent of the time; nothing does. Situational Flirting is not a quick-fix kind of thing. Not all women are going to be receptive to humor; some will get scared and stay scared. To a certain extent, it's a crapshoot. When you begin Situational Flirting with real-world women, just remember that dating is numbers game.

Women look to you for certainty that things are okay. When you're practicing Situational Flirting with a woman, you must provide a sense of certainty for her that what you're doing is okay, that there isn't any problem with you joking around with her or with her joking around with you.

Some women might be a little bit scared at first when you start doing Situational Flirting because you are definitely interrupting them on a deeper level and asking them to join you in a humorous, playful pretend reality. They are going to be looking at you, your behavior and your level of confidence and comfort to figure out whether or not there's a problem.

If you seem incredibly nervous, and come across as if you are thinking, "Oh my God, is this going to work? I'm doing a horrible thing—I'm being weird. I sure hope this doesn't wreck her day. I'm a bad guy," it will make it more likely that she will get upset. If you seem to be thinking, "Great! I'm making this joke and she is going to look to me and if I am okay with it she'll probably be okay with it too," she will more likely be fine with it.

Ultimately, if you make a Situational Flirting joke and she has a problem with it, remember: it's a numbers game and her problems are hers, so what else can you do?

Use your body. Using your body involves smiling, making eye contact with and putting energy and vitality into your voice. If you're frowning, scowling, looking at the floor or mumbling, it's going to be hard for you to get Situational Flirting to work for you. Smile, breathe, look at her and give it your best shot!

Practice, practice, practice. Situational Flirting is complicated enough that you probably won't master it overnight. If you're used to trying to control conversations with women, and most unsuccessful seducers are, it may take some practice before you get used to letting go of controlling the conversational outcomes and making creative misinterpretations and asking outrageous questions.

To succeed at Situational Flirting, you need to be in the flow of the moment, not trying to control where the interaction might take the two of you. It's risky and will take time to get used to, so give yourself 10 or 20 tries at this before expecting it to feel natural.

Be ready for a variety of responses. When we started practicing Situational Flirting, sometimes we ended up with women staring at us like they were really scared. It almost never happens now because the more we practice this flirting skill the more we trust it and the more we can project that trust and relaxation to the women we're flirting with.

Be prepared to provide both sides of the flirting interaction. Most women will be able to joke back with you; some won't. Remember when we joked about a woman's camera stealing your soul? Well, what if she didn't have any comeback at all? If so, you'd provide the comeback—something like the one you had hoped she would use. You might say, "Wait, that's not your soul-stealing camera—you must have left it at home." She can laugh at this and you'll take her off the hook for having to be clever in order to enjoy being with you.

Remember your Situational Flirting question. When you want to practice situational flirting with a woman, look around the environment you are in and ask yourself, "What is there in this situation about which I can ask some sort of outrageous or silly question? What can I creatively misinterpret in this situation that might be funny?" The answer to that question will guide you in your Situational Flirting. You'll see how we use that question in the examples below.

Learning Situational Flirting

We're going to give you examples of Situational Flirting. Please note this: These examples are going to seem silly because they are silly. You're being silly when you look at something in the environment and say something silly about it or make an outrageous joke about it. We've used all of the jokes below in real life ourselves and they've all gone quite well, so don't worry if these seem weird on the printed page.

Also remember that these examples are not prescriptions: we are not suggesting you do these exact Situational Flirting conversations. These examples are to get your mind thinking in this mode, so you can come up with your own, be flexible, and have the flirting interaction really work.

DAVID: I was recently in St. Louis and I was buying a ticket to go up in the St. Louis Arch. There was a really pretty girl selling the tickets. So I was asking myself the main question you should ask yourself for situational flirting: "What is there in this situation about which I can ask some sort of outrageous or silly question? What can I creatively misinterpret in this situation that might be funny?" So I smiled and asked her, "Do you and your friends get to go up there and party after hours in the Arch? Does it get to be your playground?" She said, "Oh yeah, we do have parties up there sometimes. You can rent it out, you know." She was nice but wasn't really getting into the joking mood yet, so I smiled and asked her, "Is it a place where you get to go a lot? Could you and me go up there sometime?" And she laughed and said, "Well, I think you should try it out with a ticket first." It was a successful flirting interaction.

David took something in the environment, the Arch itself, put an outrageous spin or interpretation on it ("Is this your personal playground?")

and got a laugh. To that woman he was funny and fun to be around and he gave her a brief, pleasurable experience. He showed her in some small way that she was special, not just an automaton dispensing tickets.

DAVID: Here's another example. I was at the *Gap* buying clothes. I don't know if you've noticed, but all the employees at the Gap wear radio headsets. I don't know if they can talk on the phone or page each other or what, but it struck me as odd, so I asked myself, "What is there in this situation about which I can ask some sort of outrageous or silly question? What can I creatively misinterpret in this situation that might be funny?" And, of course, the headsets stood out. So I asked the headset-wearing girl who was ringing me out, "Can you launch the space shuttle with that?" It wasn't very funny, but she thought it was funny enough to laugh about it.

I continued, "Oh, I know what they're doing with that headset—they are feeding you pro-Gap propaganda each and every moment, aren't they?" And she laughed and said, "Oh no! I love the Gap!" And I said, "Oh, so it's working—they've programmed you to love the Gap!" And she laughed more, and there we were, having a fun interaction together.

So the next time I come into the store I can do the same thing again. I can come in and smile and say, "Oh, so they're still feeding you that pro-Gap propaganda through your headset, right? Are you still pro-Gap?" It's become a running joke, and she and I have that little shared reality together that is different from our ordinary lives and is something that gives her pleasure. It makes it pleasurable for her to see me and she knows that I am someone she can play with. This is the kind of thing that fits in with all the flirting tools in this book.

RON: I was grocery-shopping the other day and there was a woman in the alcohol section who was pretty hot. I asked myself the question, "What is there in this situation about which I can ask some sort of outrageous or silly question? What can I creatively misinterpret in this situation that might be funny?" I thought about a misinterpretation: what if she was an undercover cop looking to arrest underage kids for trying to buy alcohol?

So I smiled and asked her, "So, what are you doing? Are you scouting for all the underage people who are trying to buy beer? You're not going to bust me, are you?" She laughed and joked back, "I don't know, you don't look too young!" I held out my wrists for her imaginary handcuffs and said, "You could bust me if you want," and we laughed together. It may look stupid when you read it here but she was loving it.

So I took the next step: I said, "My name is Ron, what's your name?" It led to something. I could have gone for her email address or phone number. If I see her again, I already have a connection with her, so it will be easy to build upon it. We have a fun imaginary world between us now. She knows she can be silly with me.

DAVID: You have probably noticed that very pretty girls often work at bookstores. I was at one such bookstore and I saw a pretty girl who worked there just sort of hanging out behind the information counter. I asked myself the question, "What is there in this situation about which I can ask some sort of outrageous or silly question? What can I creatively misinterpret in this situation that might be funny?"

So I went up to her with the book I was holding, smiled at her and said, "This book looks pretty good. Have you read it? Can you review it for me?" She said she hadn't read it, so I said, smiling and pretending to be shocked, "What, you haven't read all the books in the bookstore? I thought you knew all of the books! You look so knowledgeable there behind the information counter!" And she laughed and said, "Nope, not me! Though I do like to read, I haven't gotten to all the books yet. I'm still not even done with the literature section, and they keep adding to it!"

RON: There's a lot of stuff you can do in a bookstore. I had an experience once when I was in a bookstore and I saw a woman looking at books about UFOs. I asked myself, "What is there in this situation about which I can ask some sort of outrageous or silly question? What can I creatively misinterpret in this situation that might be funny?"

Here's what I did: smiling, I held up a book and asked, "Were you abducted by a UFO? I was abducted once. What do you think? Let's share some abduction stories." It sounds stupid, but she was laughing. It put her at ease.

In that situation, you might also "misinterpret" a woman to be an alien and say, "Wow, so are you a beautiful alien here to abduct people for tests? I'll bet that you are...are you going to take me?" It makes a joke, compliments her and shows your romantic interest. It's going to be hard for her to stuff you into the "just friends" category after you confidently told her she was beautiful during your first interaction with each other.

DAVID: Here's another example. I went into the bank, and there was a girl behind the counter, and we were doing some banking trans- action—a typical banking experience. I asked myself the question, "What is there in this situation about which I can ask some sort of outrageous or silly question? What can I creatively misinterpret in this situation that might be funny?"

And here's what I said: "So, do you get to keep a percentage of the money that comes in? You know, like a gratuity?" And she laughed and says, "Oh, that's so funny—I wish I could." Then I took our little shared fantasy one step further: "Oh, but then you would have to pay a percentage of what goes out, too. That would be bad." She laughed and said, "Oh no, I wouldn't like that part—I'd just keep the money when it comes in." I smiled and said, "That would be perfect for you! I can see it now...You get to keep the money because you do such a great job!" She said, "Yeah, that would be perfect. Here's your money, have a great day!" Next time she sees me, she'll be ready to have another fun interaction with me.

Here's another example. I was at the bank around Christmastime, and as I went up to the teller I noticed that right by her window there was a glass jar full of Tootsie Rolls with a bow around it. I looked at that candy, and asked myself the question, "What is there in this situation about which I can ask some sort of outrageous or silly question? What can I creatively misinterpret in this situation that might be funny?"

So I smiled and said, "A jar of Tootsie Rolls! Is this for me?" She said, "Well, it depends...Have you been good this year?" And I thought, "Great, she's playing along! That's wonderful." I said, "I think I've been pretty good, but in some ways I've been pretty bad, too." She laughed, and I said, "I don't know, I might need some correction as well as some rewards. Do you think you would be able to do that?" She laughed, I went on with my transaction and I left having had a successful Situational Flirting interaction.

Notice how these flirting interactions happen with women you see every day in places you go on a regular basis: the bank, the grocery store, bookstores and so on. Using this tool, you can use these places to meet and connect with women.

RON: There is one woman at my bank who I am working on. I am getting closer to asking her out by flirting with her on a regular basis. So every time I go in there, I continue a running joke Situational Flirting move I started with her weeks ago. She is just a bank teller, but I always kid her about becoming bank president. I say, "Okay, Lisa, when are they going to make you president of the bank? It's about time! I know you have been doing this work only so you can infiltrate the bank, and I know that pretty soon you are going to be the president. In fact, I am going to be your assistant..." It is just this far-out story that I keep sustaining and that we build upon every time I see her. I'll say things like "When you are the president, I will come and I will shovel the snow off your car and we'll hang out, you'll do personal loans to me, and together we'll make a killing in interest rates..."

It's easy to keep it going, and she loves it. In her day-to-day life, she probably feels like the lowest rung on the ladder—which she is—and here is a guy who actually can see her not only for what she is but in a far-out, flattering way. So that has gone really well for me.

DAVID: Restaurants are another great place to practice Situational Flirting. For instance, not too long ago I was in a bakery where they had a giveaway going: you dropped your business card in this fish bowl and if they picked it out, you won a year's worth of free bread. There was a cute girl behind the counter next to the fish bowl. I asked myself the question, "What is there in this situation about which I can ask some sort of outrageous or silly question? What can I creatively misinterpret in this situation that might be funny?"

I said to her, "So, you're going to give me a year's worth of free bread, huh?" She said, "Sure, if you win." I said, "Let me picture this now: you're going to pull up in a gigantic truck and dump a year's worth of bread on my lawn?" She laughed at the image and said, "No, no, I won't be doing it!" I said, "Oh, so somebody else will be dumping the bread on my lawn and you will be like the figure in the background who makes it happen but doesn't really come to deliver it herself?" She laughed and said, "No, no, the bread will come once a week." And so I created that humorous interaction with a woman by asking myself what I could creatively misinterpret into an outrageous, funny question.

RON: Here's another example from a coffee shop. I was sitting in a coffee shop reading the book *You Just Don't Understand.* It's about men's and women's relationship and communication issues. I'm sitting there reading this book and it is boring me, so I started asking the woman sitting at the next table what she thought about all of these examples. I'd ask her things like "It says women feel like men try to fix them instead of listening. Do you think that's true? Has that been true for you?" It turned out to be an hour-long conversation, and I got her number and email and ended up dating her. That all came out of asking her a silly question from the book, eliciting her opinion and talking. Then, all of a sudden, we were connected.

In this example, Ron didn't even "misinterpret" anything. He was simply willing to take what was in the environment and amplify it a little. He was asking himself if the examples in the book he was reading were true. Then he took his curiosity and asked the woman at the next table.

In a way, that's what all of this is about. When you do Situational Flirting, you take what is in the environment and make it a little bigger, a little more fanciful, until it becomes a little world in which you and a woman can enter together. You can learn to do this with practice.

Your Situational Flirting can be truly outrageous. Just keep asking your-self, "What is there in this situation about which I can ask some sort of outrageous or silly question? What can I creatively misinterpret in this situation that might be funny?" The opportunities really are everywhere.

For instance, if you're drinking a cup of coffee with a woman, you could look at the grounds in the bottom of the cup and say something like "I heard that some people can tell your fortune by looking at your coffee grounds...it's sort of like astrology. People do it in Turkey. Would you like me to read your fortune? Would you read mine?" If you're drinking tea, you can ask, "Would you read my tea leaves for me? I want to find out about love." She will laugh, and that is a funny, romantic thing.

This doesn't even have to be a big deal. When you're leaving a restau-rant and your pretty waitress asks you, "Do you want your receipt?" You can say, "Well, yes, I am going to take this as a memento of our time together. I'll keep it forever." If you smile while you do it, there's a good chance she'll laugh, and you'll have had a Situational Flirting interaction.

Situational Flirting is not necessarily about getting her phone number (or email address) right then and there, although you can certainly use it to get her number. It is more about being a guy who knows how to flirt, because flirting, combined with saying hi, combined with asking "What's the story behind that?," combined with the Romantic Questions, combined with giving risks, combined with everything else in this book, is what not only gets you a date but gets you a date with a woman who has been primed and tested and who is more than likely ready to be romantic or even sexual with you well before the date even happens.

DAVID: Here's another example of Situational Flirting. This is at a dentist's office. I was getting my teeth cleaned—and if that's something you haven't done in six months or so, you should probably call up your dentist and make an appointment. The receptionist was a very pretty girl. As she was checking me in, I asked her, "Are you the guardian of this bad, evil place?" She said, "Oh yeah, I'm the guardian all right." I said, "Well, can you put a spell on me, oh guardian, so the work on my teeth won't hurt?" She said, "Well, I don't know." So I said, "Okay, how about you put a spell on me so that the teeth cleaning won't hurt?" She giggled and said, "Okay, I'll put a spell on you. But I think you will still want to try the Novocain." So I came back with, "Well, I don't know. I am pretty bewitched by you already, but okay." We had this wonderful joking conversation about how she had this magical power and it was fun for us both.

RON: I can think of one example of Situational Flirting that David and I did together every time we saw a certain woman at our local co-op grocery store. She was kind of punky-looking and would wear army fatigues most of the time. So we nicknamed her the General, and every time we went there we would salute her: "Hello General, how are you today? What are our orders?" She would just crack up.

We had a running joke about her being an army spy. We'd ask her, "Are you here spying or are you here for some covert operation?" And she would say, "Yep, I'm here spying." We'd say something like "So, you're here to see what is going on in this store in case you have to make a tactical move, right?" And she'd say something like "I'd tell you, but I'd have to kill you." It was really fun, and when we'd come in, her eyes would light up and she would really look forward to talking to us.

Here's another example: We were in New York City on a beautiful spring day once doing some promotion for one of our books and we were walking down the street and these three beautiful women came out of this nail spa. They had just had their nails done and they were admiring them, and I said to them, "Oh, it's the beautiful nail women! You must be here to show the world your beautiful nails. Can we see?" They were thrilled to show us their new nails. We told them how beautiful they looked and how beautiful their nails looked and they were laughing and giggling. We joked about how they must be getting ready to be in an international nail contest and they thought it was great. It was really fun for us too.

Here are some places where you can try out your Situational Flirting skills today:

- The health club
- The mall
- The bank or credit union
- The coffee shop
- The video store
- The subway or train
- A bar
- A restaurant
- A bookstore
- A shop
- A line
- Anywhere else you find yourself

Basically, anywhere you encounter a woman you should be asking your-self, "What is there in this situation about which I can ask some sort of outrageous or silly question? What can I creatively misinterpret in this situation that might be funny?"

CONCLUSION

Situational Flirting accomplishes a number of worthy goals:

When you practice Situational Flirting with a woman, you show that you're not just a friend because you're playing with her in a way that a lowly male friend never would.

You're interrupting her at a deeper level and injecting yourself into her consciousness. This shows her that you're the kind of guy who can go after what he wants and can make things happen.

You provide pleasure for the woman. You create a little make-believe world together, which is a welcome relief from the difficulty and tedium of her normal life.

Situational Flirting also brings out a playful part of yourself, which is sexy to women. Remember, silliness and sexiness have a close relation-ship. When you flirt and are silly with a woman and provide her with reassurance that things are okay, you become sexier to her.

Finally, you provide a fun experience for yourself. When you have fun with a woman, you leave the interaction charged up, with higher self-esteem and more energy than when you started.

As you get better and better at Situational Flirting, you'll find that it creates a self-reinforcing cycle: the more you practice it with women, the more energy you have, and the more you want to do it with women. And that's good. •

CHapter 8
Deepening

We're now going to take flirting to the next level with a process called Deepening. Deepening is a way of taking anything a woman says to you and turning it into a bonding conversation. Deepening is about having an intimate talk and developing rapport.

This is part of a series of steps that leads to asking a woman out and getting the date. Hi leads to asking "What's the story behind that?" which can lead to Deepening. Deepening then moves into Romantic Conversations and asking for the number. When you feel comfortable with this progression and have some experience trying it out on women, you'll quickly become a pro.

What exactly is Deepening? Deepening is a conversational mode that allows you to get into a woman's world and find out what she's passionate about. Deepening is a way for you to acknowledge, and help her acknowledge, what she cares about. Deepening is powerful because most women aren't used to being recognized in ways that feel romantic. Most women don't see themselves as special and aren't used to other people seeing them as special. When you're able to see the passionate and special parts of a woman and feed it back to her, she'll feel a bond with you. With Deepening, you can develop a connection with a woman without bamboozling her.

THE TWO COMPONENTS OF DEEPENING

- You ask a woman questions about her passions and interests.
- Based on what she tells you, you describe her passions and interests for her so she feels acknowledged and sees the details of her life in a new and positive way.

THE FIVE BASIC RULES OF DEEPENING

Focus on what a woman is passionate about. The purpose of Deepening is to look for areas in a woman's life where she feels passion and feed it back to her. You are validating aspects of her life that most people do not see or acknowledge. When you show a woman that she's special, she will feel appreciative and bond with you.

Pay attention to details. Pay attention to the details of what the woman is saying and look for ways to feed back those details to her in a romantic way.

Avoid the Deepening trap. When you are asking a woman Deepening Questions, sometimes she'll mention negative aspects of her life. It's important to avoid topics that she is upset about. When bad things come up, redirect the conversation to what is working in her life and what she's most interested in.

Always include the Romantic Moves. To insure that you come across as a romantic possibility, you need to use the Romantic Moves. If you hold eye contact "too long," make decisions quickly and easily, wink at a woman, check out her body, compliment her, keep your body powerful and whisper to her, your chances of having a successful Deepening Conversation are greatly increased.

This is only a test... When you conduct a Deepening conversation, you are testing to see if a woman might be someone you want to go out with. You are testing to see if she likes you and if you like her. Eventually, you'll either talk about topics she's passionate about or you should probably end the conversation and move on to someone else.

Be on the lookout for openings to ask for a date, phone number, or email address. Watch for chances to ask for these things. The goal of Deepening is for women to have positive experiences with you, have them expose parts of themselves to you that they rarely expose to anyone else and then have them feel enough safety and rapport to go out with you.

Deepening Conversation 1

DAVID: Here's a recent example of a Deepening Conversation I had at a party. I was talking to a woman and asked her a simple question.

DAVID: So what do you do for a living?

CASSIE: I'm a social worker.

DAVID: Wow, that's really interesting. You must see all sorts of things in a job like that.

CASSIE: Yes, I do.

DAVID: Where do you work?

CASSIE: I work down at the hospital.

DAVID: Let me ask you a question. In every job there are aspects that you dislike and moments when you feel like you really don't like what you are doing, but then there are moments when you feel like you really are doing what you were put on earth to do. I would be curious to know, if you would care to share, what are some of those moments for you?

CASSIE: Well, I help the families of children who are getting organ transplants. I do all the coordinating and I also deal with all of their emotions.

DAVID: That's really incredible.

CASSIE: Yes, it's an amazing job. And there are times when I am working with families and I really do feel like you said, like I am doing what I was put on earth here to do. I get the surgery and the organs coordinated. I get the kids ready and I get the families ready and it is like I become a member of their family for a while.

DAVID: Wow, that is really incredible. You must really be a woman who values making a difference in people's lives.

CASSIE: I really do, that is what I really love about my job.

DAVID: I don't get to see that kind of a thing in a woman every day. I really appreciate seeing that in you, it's really inspiring to me.

CASSIE: Wow, that is really great that you see that too...

RON: Let's talk about this example. You got her talking about what she is most passionate about and then you restated it back to her, which is how Deepening works. It's a good example of starting with a simple question and having the conversation become more intimate and personal. From there, David could have built up to asking for her phone number or asking for the date.

DAVID: In this Deepening Conversation I was able to get a lot of information from her. She seemed very interested in talking to me and gave lengthy answers to each of my questions.

Deepening Conversation 2: at a Yoga Class

DAVID: What do you do?

SOPHIE: I'm an accountant.

DAVID: I find accounting interesting. In my business I've been studying some accounting lately. It must really feel amazing when you are able line up all those numbers and all those columns. It must feel incredible when you have everything balanced and everything is perfectly in order.

SOPHIE: Yes, that's exactly what it's like.

DAVID: Let's talk about this example. In this example I came up with a way to feed back to her the excitement of those best moments in accounting. When I fed that back to her I was able to see something in her life that most guys do not see. Most guys would have said something like "So, what kind of software do you use as an accountant?" But I was able to see the magic of having all the numbers line up. When I reflected her passion back to her, her eyes got big and shiny.

RON: One thing that I want to highlight in David's example is that he took a risk when he described to the accountant what might be exciting about her job. I like that he said, "I finally found an angle that I thought might work." Let's underline the phrase "might work." When you are having Deepening Conversations, you're going to be taking risks and trying things out and sometimes falling flat on your face. David and I have enough experience, and have failed enough, that we have a clue of what might work and what might not work, but the only way for you to get to a place where you know what works is through trial and error.

DAVID: With both of my examples, I could have chosen to ask less intimate questions—questions that would have made me more of a friend than a romantic possibility. With the social worker, for example, I could have said, "Oh, where do you work? Is that a good job? Wow, what are the hours like?" Those would have been questions that would have kept me in the friend zone. Instead I asked, "What is it about that that makes you passionate, that makes you feel turned on?" When I met the accountant, I came back with, "It must feel incredible when you have everything balanced." She said, "Yes."

It's important to remember that some women hate their jobs. So if you ask, "What do you do for a living?" a woman might say something like, "I work for a dentist. I am his receptionist and I really hate it." Then if you ask her if there is anything she likes about her job, she's likely to say, "No." If that happens, here's how to handle it. We recommend you say, "Okay, I would be curious to know, if you are willing to share, what is it that you are passionate about? What is it in your life, if it is not your job, and for a lot of us it really isn't our job, that really turns you on as a woman and makes you feel like you are really doing something you love?"

Deepening Conversation 3

Ron talked to a woman recently who told him she hated her job. So he knew to avoid asking her about it. Instead, he asked what she's most passionate about in her life.

KATE: I love animals and I volunteer at the pet shelter.

RON: That's interesting. What are the best moments when you're volunteering at the pet shelter?

KATE: Some of the best moments for me are when a dog comes in and they are sick and I am able to work with them and nurse them back to health. I spend time with them and then a family comes in and adopts them. It makes me really happy when everything works out well. It makes me feel like I have made a difference in the world.

RON: Wow, I can see you are a woman who really values making a difference, and that's wonderful.

KATE: Yeah, I really do value helping people. Thank you, that's nice to hear you say that.

RON: Well, I don't meet women every day who are so focused on helping people. I think that's really special and I can see that you are a special woman.

RON: The point of this example is that a Deepening Conversation can go well when you ask a woman what she's passionate about in her life and avoid focusing on her job. Asking a woman what she's passionate about in her life is a good way to shift the topic whenever she mentions that her job sucks. It's a good technique to use when a woman starts talking about any aspect of her life that is difficult, stressful or challenging. You can easily move on to more pleasant topics by asking her what she's passionate about.

Deepening Conversation 4

DAVID: So Heidi, you seem interesting to talk to. I'd be curious to know what you do for a living?

HEIDI: I'm a writer and a cook. I cook for a couple of people who are really busy. Both of my jobs are pretty fun.

DAVID: That sounds interesting. What do you like to write about?

HEIDI: I write about cooking, health and current events. Sometimes I review restaurants, sometimes I write about cooking and other times I write about health issues. One of the best parts of my job is that I travel and write freelance articles for travel magazines. All of my interests tie together.

RON: Let's stop for a second. How is the conversation going, David?

DAVID: I'm happy with it at this point. As we examine additional examples of Deepening, you'll see how we go from asking what she does for a living to what she's passionate about. I already asked Heidi what she likes to write about, which is a way to start exploring what she's passionate about. By my asking personal questions, she sees me as a guy who is interested in what she has to say and who cares about her life.

RON: A big part of Deepening is paying attention to details. Romance is in the details. It would have been easy for David to say, "Oh, you're a cook and you write, what else do you like to do?" Instead of overlooking the details and asking mundane, general questions, David was able to dig deeper into specific interests of Heidi's and feed them back to her.

Let's go back and look at more of David's conversation.

DAVID: I see how it all kind of fits together, the cooking, the traveling and writing about restaurants and food. That's interesting, it is almost as if there is this whole lifestyle around cooking and writing for you.

HEIDI: Yes, that's very much what my life is about. Those are my key interests and I am glad that's also how I make my living.

DAVID: I know that in every kind of job or career there are parts of it that kind of suck. Maybe it sucks to be washing the dishes or cleaning a kitchen, but I also know there are other moments that are really stellar—moments where you really feel like this is what you were put on this earth to do. I would be curious to know what some of those moments are for you.

RON: I want to butt in here again. One of the classic David lines is what he just asked Heidi. It's a great phrase.

DAVID: Here's another question I recommend: "What might be one of those moments where you feel the work you are doing is really turning you on?" When you ask that question or the one I just put to Heidi, the woman you're talking to will have to start exploring her life in a new way. Let's look at the conversation some more.

HEIDI: Like I said before, I really like to travel, and it's great that I can travel so frequently. I really enjoy meeting new people and seeing new places. Sometimes I am flying somewhere and I think, "Wow, I am getting paid to do this."

DAVID: You are making a contribution to people's lives, too. In both the foods you are cooking and in your writing you're making a difference in people's health.

HEIDI: That's true. I am really interested in health and nutrition. I like teaching people about it because I believe the emotional, physical and spiritual aspects of life are all connected.

DAVID: That's cool. I've done a lot of cooking myself.

HEIDI: That's great!

DAVID: When I am cooking a meal, it's nice to be in a kitchen where everything is humming along. You've got all these different pots of food cooking, all the ingredients are cut up and you really feel like you are on top of it all.

HEIDI: I love that feeling. That's a good way to describe what it's like to be cooking a multi-course meal.

DAVID: Sometimes I've got a zillion things going and I'm doing one thing with one hand and something else with another. There are many pots of food all cooking and each pot is cooking at a different temperature and everything is going along just perfectly. I sometimes just get lost in the process.

HEIDI: Yes, that's a wonderful feeling.

RON: Let's jump in and make some comments about where this conversation is going.

DAVID: I told Heidi that she contributes to people's lives through her writing and her cooking. I decided that it was more powerful to look at how she contributes to people's lives rather than asking what she likes to cook or some less personal question. From there I was able to admire the fact that she makes a difference in people's lives and then feed it back to her.

RON: In these examples of Deepening you can see how we are able to describe to women the exciting parts of their lives in ways they do not usually see. We are validating something that they don't normally associate with themselves. When we acknowledge those things, like David did with Heidi, we bond with the women.

DAVID: I want to point out that I took a risk when I told her that I am interested in cooking. As a general rule, you should limit how much you share about yourself, at first. It never ceases to amaze me how often I rediscover that women are not interested in men during the initial conversations.

I decided that it was okay to mention that I am into cooking because I thought it would be a bonding detail. I also thought I could use my interest in cooking as a springboard to start describing good feelings associated with cooking. So I talked about how good it feels to have several things cooking at once and how easy it is to get lost in the process.

RON: Yes, that was a good segue for her to talk about her experience as a cook. Since you are actually into cooking it was a good move. There is no reason to lie or even be misleading to get women into your life or into your bed.

DAVID: When I mentioned all the pots going at once and being in the flow of cooking, I knew she would relate to that description. When she responded, I could see her eyes light up, and she smiled.

When you are able conduct a Deepening Conversation and include the Romantic Moves, you will really stand out from other men. Let's continue on with the conversation and see where it goes.

HEIDI: It's actually like putting on a show or something, because you have all these little components coming together at once. I cooked in restaurants for years and often had the experience of people working together to prepare something wonderful to eat. I know exactly that feeling you're talking about.

DAVID: I've noticed that there is a flow when I am cooking; it's almost like you're dancing with it. There is also the moment with the presentation where you are actually putting the food out. I don't know if you ever think about putting the food on the plate and how beautiful it looks on the table.

HEIDI: Oh yes, I am really picky about that. When I used to cook in a restaurant, I didn't let anyone else do the finishing of the dish. I think it is really important for me to have it balanced visually and to have a nice color contrast going on with the different foods that are on the plate. It is definitely an artistic thing and I really express myself through the presentation of food.

DAVID: Those moments are really special. There is all the setup and all the preparation, and then you take a second and look at all the food and feel all the effort you just put into creating something wonderful. You realize that in 20 minutes the food will be gone, but there is that perfect moment just before you serve the food. Do you know what I'm saying?

HEIDI: Yes, I do. I've had that experience frequently in my life and it's really special. It's really exhilarating.

DAVID: I can see that artist in you. I see the artistry in getting the food perfect for people and the artistic presentation. A wonderful meal is something so creative and really gives people an experience. The right meal is so memorable. You put together a meal, you put it in front of your guests and it is perfect in every way. You've made a real contribution, which is great.

RON: Let's jump in again. So how are things going, David?

DAVID: I'm happy with how things are going. I see that the conversation has gotten more intense and we're getting along well. First off, there was talk about how great it feels to be in a kitchen. In the back of my mind I was saying, "Well, I know I want her to be feeling a sense of connection to me, and I'm seeing things in her life that she doesn't get to share with most people." So I asked myself what else in the area of cooking might be a moment where she would feel those really good feelings? When I asked myself that question, I decided to mention that the moment of presentation is a moment where you might feel really good. So I asked her about the presentation. Heidi seemed to get off on that question. I told her, "I can see that artist in you." She responded positively to that.

You can see that Deepening is not gimmicky stuff. You can tell from Heidi's comments that she values art, creativity and self-expression. I am not using cheesy lines with Heidi, I'm trying to find ways to make a deeper connection.

By the way, my conversation with Heidi will continue in the next chapter.

Deepening Conversation 5

DAVID: Now let's look at a short conversation between me and Megan. This conversation is a great example of Deepening and goes through the Deepening structure we've been teaching you. I start by asking Megan about her job, and the conversation unfolds nicely from there.

DAVID: What do you do in your life that really inspires you?

MEGAN: It's really important to me to have jobs that inspire me. For years I had a job that I just loved. I was in charge of a small-town Chamber of Commerce, and they thrived on tourism. I had a ball working there, coming up with new ideas and promoting the town.

DAVID: It sounds like there were a lot of moments in that job where you really felt like you were doing what you were put on earth to do.

MEGAN: Yes, I constantly felt like I was doing my life's work. When I had a new idea, everyone got behind it and implemented it. Sometimes the job was really difficult. Sometimes the people in the community were hard to work with or there would be unexpected problems. In the end, however, when each project was over, everyone was always happy and I was responsible for all the success.

DAVID: That's a great feeling when you have finished a big project. It's wonderful to look at all the work that you did behind the scenes, the things that no one will even know you did, and see what an accomplishment it is to complete such a great project.

MEGAN: All those nights I would be up late, counting things or putting packets together, I always felt like it was all worth it in the end.

DAVID: That is really great.

RON: Let's jump in here. Your thoughts, David?

DAVID: When you're just getting to know a woman it often makes sense to talk about safe and gentle subjects and then later build into heavier, more romantic talk. We want to reiterate that Deepening conversations are all about creating a connection with a woman that has her feel like you see something in her that most people do not see. Being able to see things in a woman that most men don't see creates an emotional connection. With Megan I wanted to focus on talking about her job and on getting to know her as a way to start the bonding process.

Deepening conversation 6

In this conversation, look at how Ron keeps deepening the conversation with Terri. Ron gets away with being very direct with Terri. Depending on your personality, being silly, obnoxious and sort of pushy with women might work. What makes this example with Ron work is that he is playful with Terri but only acts silly in the context of rapport building. He continues to ask her questions about what's important to her and what she's passionate about. You can get away with being a bad boy when you combine making a connection, being respectful, having fun and pushing the limits all at once. When you only joke around and only act obnoxiously, a woman will not connect with you.

RON: What are you passionate about in your life?

TERRI: Music is one thing I really like. I recently started singing and I'm also learning how to play the guitar.

RON: That's great. I love the guitar and I've been playing for a long time. I don't meet many women who are aspiring guitar pros.

TERRI: I just love music. A friend of mine is a guitar player and wanted me to start learning so we could play together. I thought the guitar might be more fun than the drums.

RON: I play guitar, so I know what that is like when you are playing and you get lost in the music and you feel like "this is great" and you lose yourself for a few moments in the music.

TERRI: Yes, I know what it feels like to lose myself in music. I have a question for you, did you sing with other people when you were playing?

RON: Yeah, I played in bands for a long time. I was also a touring musician for a few years.

DAVID: I want to jump in here for a moment and look at how Ron went quickly went from talking about music to talking about the moment where you are playing music and getting lost in the process. He is looking for moments where Terri feels passionate. He is taking what she's talking about, which is music, and looking for ways to feed it back to her in a romantic manner. Let's go back and read more.

RON: The act of playing music is a lot of fun. You know the feeling of getting lost in music and being able to spontaneously create something really beautiful?

TERRI: Yeah, I have written some songs and it's fun.

RON: That's great that you've been able to write music.

DAVID: Let's break in here again for a second. Ron talks about getting lost in music and she does not really answer. So he goes back and tries to ask her a similar question. Ron displays tenacity in that he has to keep guiding the conversation into romantic spaces no matter how Terri replies. When you are having Deepening Conversations, it's important that you keep guiding a woman toward passionate conversations and passionate topics. Eventually, you'll either successfully turn the conversation to something she's passionate about or you'll probably want to stop talking to her. Let's look at some more:

RON: That's great that you've been able to write music.

TERRI: I really enjoy writing music and I'm focused much more on music these days than on my job. Music just really juices me up these days.

RON: Do you go see live music a lot?

Terri: I don't see many live bands right now. I've mostly been focusing on learning how to play the guitar and also on creating my own music. I've been really unhappy with my job these days, but music has been really fun.

RON: All right, set the mood for me. Let's say you invite me over to listen to you sing and play guitar. Let's say you invite me over for a private listening party, what would the mood of it be? What's the experience like for you when you are sitting there listening to music that you love?

DAVID: Let's jump in. How is this conversation going for you at this point, Ron?

RON: At this point I am trying to make the big shift into asking for her phone number and/or asking for the date. We've talked about music and I feel like our rapport is pretty good. So now I want to try to test her and see how receptive she is to the idea of me coming over to her place. If she's unreceptive I will go back in and do more Deepening, and if she's open I will ask for the number. Another advantage of testing Terri by asking how she'd feel to have me over to her place is that it takes the conversation to a much deeper area.

DAVID: Another thing Ron did in that segment of the conversation was to avoid the trap of asking her why her job sucks. Many of us fall into the trap of trying to be compassionate man and caring by asking her about work problems. Having a woman talk about areas of her life that are not going well is generally a bad idea. It is a way to kill a seduction. Luckily, Ron avoids that trap and starts looking at what it would be like for Terri to have him over to her house. This is where he starts pushing the limits.

RON: I wanted to ask her a playful and silly question so that if she didn't want to go out with me my comments would sound like a joke. At the same time, if she is interested in me she knows that I am interested in going out with her. I like testing women in a humorous manner because I learn a lot about where I should take the conversation next.

Let's listen to Terri's answer:

TERRI: My choice in music really changes a lot. If I am playing guitar and singing then it's probably folksy, acoustic music, nothing fancy. That's the style of music I like playing the most.

RON: Okay, let's set the scene again. You've invited me to your place and you are serenading me and I am watching you closely. That sounds wonderful.

TERRI: Are you going to sing along?

RON: Not at this second, but I would if I was with you at your place.

TERRI: Do you know harmony? Can you sing harmony with me?

RON: Sure, that'd be great!

TERRI: Can you help me operate my four-track recorder? I haven't figured out how to use it and I'd like to record myself singing some of the songs I've written. Are you good with recording equipment?

RON: I've done quite a bit of recording and would have fun playing around with your four-track machine. I could come over and help you if you want me to.

DAVID: As you can see Ron was working to nail down a date with her. He said, "I could come over and help you if you want me to." It seems like their conversation is heading towards a date and Terri seems receptive to going out with him. She's asking Ron if he can sing harmony and she's wondering if he knows how to use recording equipment—all good signs. You can also see that he's not acting like a friend, there's a romantic feel about the conversation.

In the next chapter, we'll look at several more conversations and learn Advanced Deepening skills. But let's go over what you've learned so far. The Deepening process seems pretty simple when you read about it, but conducting a Deepening Conversation can sometimes be confusing. Here are some key points to remember:

Review of Guidelines for Deepening Conversations

Focus on what a woman is passionate about. The purpose of Deepening is to look for areas in a woman's life where she feels passion and feed it back to her. You are validating aspects of her life that most people do not see or acknowledge. When you show a woman that she's special, she will feel appreciative and bond with you.

Pay attention to details. Pay attention to the details of what the woman is saying and look for ways to feed back those details to her in a romantic way.

Avoid the Deepening trap. As we mentioned before, when you are asking a woman Deepening Questions, sometimes she'll mention negative aspects of her life. It's important to avoid topics that she is upset about. When bad things come up, redirect the conversation to what is working in her life and what she's most interested in.

Always include the Romantic Moves. As we also said before, to insure that you come across as a romantic possibility, you need to use the Romantic Moves. If you hold eye contact too long, make decisions quickly and easily, wink at a woman, check out her body, compliment a woman, keep your body powerful and whisper to her, your chances of having a successful Deepening Conversation are greatly increased.

This is only a test... In these examples, you can see how Ron and David were testing the woman's attraction and receptivity by using the Deepening conversational structure to push things a little. You should do this, too.

THE TOP THREE DEEPENING QUESTIONS

- A good way to start a Deepening Conversation is to ask a woman what she does for a living. This is a low-pressure question and most women will feel comfortable answering it.
- David's Deepening Question: "I know that in every kind of job or career there are parts of it that kind of suck and other moments are really stellar where you really feel like this is what you were put on this earth to do. You know those moments where you reach the

peak, where you feel totally turned on? I would be curious to know, if you would care to share, what are some of those moments for you?"

- Another simple question to ask a woman is "What are you most passionate about in your life?"

CONCLUSION

Here are two things you can do to start using this skill in your interactions with women:

- Look for opportunities to have Deepening Conversations and start asking some of the Deepening Questions.
- Start to ask "What do you do for a living?" and "What is it that you find really touches your heart? I know some moments are really difficult but there are these moments where you feel like you were put here on earth to do that thing. What are those moments for you?" Experiment, and start having Deepening Conversations.•

How to Talk to Women

CHAPTER 9
ADVANCED DEEPENING

In this chapter we'll continue to provide examples of Deepening Conversations. We'll also include several Advanced Deepening Skills. By the end of this chapter you'll be crystal clear on how to initiate and manage Deepening Conversations. In the next chapter, we'll show you how to move from Deepening Conversations to Romantic Conversations.

In this chapter you will get a much clearer sense of how to move from Deepening Conversations to asking for phone numbers and how to take the seduction to the next level.

Here's a preview of the Advanced Deepening Skills you're going to learn in this chapter:

- Why Deepening Conversations with women sometimes fail
- How to include yourself when describing scenes to a woman
- How and why you must assume rapport
- The importance of having fun when talking to women
- How to ask open-ended questions
- How to evoke information that a woman would never share with a stranger
- How to use Deepening Conversations to create a connection
- How to use Deepening to admire women

- How to ask women about great moments in their lives
- How to use Advanced Deepening Questions like "What are you most passionate about?" and "What are the postcard moments that you will remember for the rest of your life?"
- Why you should avoid pushing a woman during Deepening Conversations
- The importance of "you" statements
- How to take on a "you" point of view
- Why you must shut up and listen
- How Deepening is like fishing
- What to do if women turn the tables on you
- How Deepening Conversations can lead to touching or kissing
- How asking "What's the best part of it?" can often save the day

So here we go: lights, camera, more Deepening!

Deepening Conversation 7

RON: This is a conversation with Sue. Note how I go from asking her what she's passionate about to moving the conversation into a romantic and sexy direction. This conversation is a good example of how quickly you can move from simple Deepening Questions to romantic talk.

RON: Sue, what is it that you are passionate about? You mentioned earlier that you are interested in art and also into being a biker babe, but I am curious about your other interests. What else are you passionate about in your life?

SUE: I have to go back to the arts because that is my favorite thing. I like to go to art openings, art shows and I am a very progressive person. I like all kinds of art but especially modern art. I like being creative and I like creative people. I also enjoy live music and have a wide range of musical interests, from classical to jazz and blues.

RON: I'm a big music fan too. Do you frequently go see live music?

SUE: I go to as many concerts as I can.

RON: Would going to a concert be something you'd consider a fun date?

DAVID: Let's jump in here. Sue gave Ron a lot of information and he instantly moved in a romantic direction with that last question. He is learning information about her interests and planting the idea in her head that they might go on a date.

RON: I am also assuming rapport, which is really crucial. I am assuming that she's into talking to me and into being with me. It's crucial to assume the best when you're with a woman. Many of our students are so used to having conversations with women go poorly that they always assume the worst. When you assume a woman doesn't like you and is not enjoying being with you, you come across as awkward and uncomfortable. When you're talking to women, do your best to assume rapport and your confidence will improve.

In Deepening, we're looking at what a woman is passionate about and interested in. So early on I am focused on finding out Sue's interests and passions. It is obvious that she is into art, creativity, music, so I want to connect those topics to me. Sue seems very open and flirtatious and there is a lot of eye contact, so I want to bring up romantic topics right away. Many of our students wait too long before pushing conversations in a romantic direction. Our students often think they need to wait until the end of a conversation to bring up romantic topics, but it's often better to bring up romantic topics early on. If there is a space to ask Romantic Questions, go for it.

To turn up the romance with Sue, I asked her what a great date would look like to her. I wanted to ask her questions that create openings for me to ask her out. I also wanted to ask her questions that would quickly show me whether or not she'd be open to going out with me.

THE FOUR-STEP ADVANCED DEEPENING DESCRIPTION PROCESS

Instead of describing a great concert or a wonderful piece of art, in Advanced Deepening, you describe a situation where you and she are together at a concert or an art museum. Instead of describing a fun art gallery or museum, you describe a scene where both of you are at an art gallery or museum looking at art. Instead of describing a romantic candlelit dinner, you describe a romantic dinner where the two of you are drinking wine and having a great time.

When you describe romantic scenes with the two of you, it's just one more way for her to start imagining you as a potential lover. The process goes like this:

- Pick a situation you want to describe, such as a fun date, a great trip, a vacation or a concert.

- Imagine that you are describing her in that situation and add details to the scene to make it more intimate. If you learn that she's into art, you could ask yourself what about being in an art gallery would make it more intimate. Perhaps you imagine drinking wine at an art opening and getting lost in a conversation. Maybe you imagine looking at the art and appreciating its beauty. Maybe you imagine it's an elegant art opening and everyone looks so beautiful and you just look at each other and smile and feel so happy. Whatever the scene, you add intimate details.

- Put yourself in the scene. The imaginary scene would feature the two of you at an elegant art opening, both looking great and really having a fun time. Or maybe both of you are drinking wine at an art opening and having a fun time laughing and smiling at each other and laughing at all the pretentious people. Or maybe both of you are staring at the beautiful art on the walls and getting lost in it together.

- Now describe this scene to the woman. Yes, you eventually have to take the risk to talk. You need to open your mouth and create some of these situations when talking to the woman you are with.

After you have some clues about the things a woman is interested in, we recommend you follow this four-step sequence a few times during each Deepening Conversation.

Deepening Conversation 7 continued

When we left off with this chat, Ron had just asked if Sue thought going to a concert would be a fun date.

SUE: I'd enjoy going to a concert. I'd even enjoy just going to a bar and listening to some live blues. Nothing is more fun than having fun, drinking and dancing your feet off.

RON: Well, what about going on rides on the back of a Harley?

SUE: I think that would be great too. I'm an adventurous person and I love bikes. So my idea of a good time would be to just get in the car, or get on a bike if it is a nice night, and just head out some-where and maybe just go all night and fall asleep where we end up—maybe just sleep outside under the stars. I think that would be so much fun.

DAVID: Let's jump in. How is this going?

RON: I am getting a lot of useful information from Sue. I am asking questions and getting information on where to possibly take her on a date. I am also asking her questions that will have her think of going out with me. Lastly, I am having fun talking to her.

Having fun when talking to a woman is really important. If a con-versation is not fun it's often a sign that the woman is not interest-ed in you. Whenever you're not having fun it's important to ask yourself what's not working. Are you nervous? Are you trying too hard to get into her pants? Is she boring you so badly you want to leave? What's going on in your mind and what can you do that second to start having fun? Having fun, being sexy, being interested and being interesting all work together.

Let's listen in some more:

RON: You've convinced me. I am ready to take you out, and we leave tonight. It's our secret operation.

SUE: [Laughs] I want to explore the whole world, which is my passion. I have a goal to travel around the world before I die.

RON: Where have you traveled? I don't meet a lot of women who really go for what they want. I meet a lot of women who want to go for it, but most don't have the guts to go out and really do it.

SUE: I have been to Europe and Mexico, but I really want to go to Asia and Australia. The next trip I am planning is to visit Asia.

DAVID: Let's jump in again. Is there anything you want to say, Ron?

RON: I was feeling closer and closer to asking her out. I was happy with the pace and depth of the conversation. Sue seemed to be having a good time talking to me and we were bonding.

I used humor to connect with her. Turning a date into a secret operation made it more fun and exciting. I took the conversation into a different direction and in the process we both had fun. Women like to go on adventures and they like it when you can be playful. When you can create dates that are adventures, you'll come across as seductive, romantic and fun.

Deepening Conversation 8

In this conversation David uses the Deepening Questions you've been learning.

We want to warn you ahead of time that Laura is an odd woman, but very attractive. She talks about wanting to simplify her life and at times comes across like a survivalist. Are there a lot of weird women out there? Yes! Are there women who are interested in topics you find stupid, boring and insane? Yes! Are there women who will say things and give opinions you strongly disagree with? Yes! So it's important that we include some women in this book who are a bit odd and off-kilter since you're likely to encounter them in your own dating life.

In talking to random women you will encounter women who seem odd to you. We all encounter women who say unusual things. Our task is to decide if they're worth pursuing. If so, we need to stop focusing on the unusual aspects of their personalities. Once you're pursuing a woman, harboring negative judgments about her tend to get in the way of a successful seduction. Once you're in a relationship, you need to ignore the aspects of a woman's personality that bother you. It's called coping with the harsh reality.

DAVID: Hi Laura, nice to see you. I'm curious—what is your job?

LAURA: I own a small hotel, but I am getting out of the hotel business to simplify my life. I also own a computer consulting company.

DAVID: Simplifying your life is such an important thing. I would guess that you are someone who values trying to simplify things when everything seems complex. Is that true?

LAURA: Absolutely, I keep working at it and always try to simplify things for myself.

DAVID: What does your vision of a simple life look like?

LAURA: Just a simple house in the country and not having to work much.

DAVID: That sounds nice and much more laid back.

RON: Let's jump in. How's this conversation going for you, David?

DAVID: At the beginning I asked her what else she would like to do in business. I wanted to throw a wide a net so she wouldn't feel cornered by my questions. You want to ask women open-ended questions and give them the room to respond how they want.

Since Laura mentioned that she was simplifying her life, I asked her about it. In the back of my mind, I was looking for something she's passionate about, and I kept asking questions until she gave me something to work with.

LAURA: I really am turned on by the idea of living in the country, being pretty self-sufficient and just being able to do whatever I want to do.

DAVID: So you really value self-sufficiency, doing what you want to do and taking it easy?

LAURA: Yes I do. I want to take a break from the rat race.

DAVID: That would be a reason to start your own business too, to create something you would be able to sell and to do exactly what you want to do. That's cool. I don't get to meet women every day that are so direct in their lives. It sounds great to live somewhere beautiful and be able to sit in the sun and have a good time.

DAVID: Let's jump in again. In the last section I spent a lot of time validating her desire to live in a secluded area and simplify her life. I want her to feel admired. In feeding back to her the qualities she values I'm seeing parts of her that most people overlook. I am taking notice of what is special to her and what is special about her. I am also listening intently to what she's saying. I am listening for useful information and concentrating on how I can turn what she's telling me into more Deepening Questions.

Deepening Conversation 4 Continued

In the previous chapter David talked to Heidi. Here's the conclusion of their conversation. In this example, David uses Deepening to get Heidi's phone number.

DAVID: How long have you been writing?

HEIDI: I've always enjoyed writing. In fact my Mom has these funny little books that I wrote when I was a kid which she held on to. It is really hilarious looking at them.

DAVID: What was one of your books about?

HEIDI: One of them was about my cat Snowball.

DAVID: Your cat Snowball?

HEIDI: Yes, it was a book full of little illustrations. It's pretty funny to look at.

DAVID: I'd like to hear about it.

HEIDI: It's made out of construction paper and each page has another little fact about my cat. I was probably 5 when I made it. Later, when I was 7 or so, I came out with a bigger book about unicorns.

DAVID: Wow, that's so cool. That's a really sweet childhood image. Do you feel that now you're able to tap into that little-kid energy when you are creating stuff and writing?

HEIDI: I tap into it sometimes. I can feel it when I am writing for myself but not usually when I am writing for work. I find myself being able to be free when I am not writing under the pressure of a deadline.

DAVID: Would you say that you get those moments where you feel like a little girl again? You know, just letting it all go and feeling happy and carefree?

HEIDI: Yes, definitely.

RON: Let's break in here again and dissect what David's done so far. Tell us what you're thinking at this point in the conversation.

DAVID: Well, I knew from my previous conversation with Heidi that she works as a writer. So I asked her about the writing. Then she told me about the books she wrote as a kid. I admired Heidi for writing those little books. When she talks about her current writing I ask her about tapping into that little-kid energy.

I am trying to focus the conversation on feelings that are open, receptive and sweet. I'm bringing up images of feeling free and happy like a little kid. You should focus on asking women about the best moments in their lives, both past and present.

When Heidi told me about the books she wrote as a kid, I said, "Wow, that's so cool." She was sharing something from her heart there, something kind of intimate. Heidi was sharing something with me that she would not necessarily share with a stranger, so I wanted to validate her for sharing those things with me.

HEIDI: I wish I could incorporate those feelings of freedom and wonder more into my professional work. Sometimes I can, but it's really fun to let that side out.

DAVID: You seem like a really interesting woman. It's really great that you're doing things in life that you're turned on by. I'm curious to know what you're most passionate about in your writing. Do you have those moments like "Wow, this is what I was put here to do" and you feel like the writing is coming through you?

HEIDI: Yes, I go through periods like that. I feel that way when I'm not thinking about the final product, not thinking about what I need to do. I feel really happy when I'm able to just enjoy the process—

when I can let go and enjoy writing. Those are also moments where I think, "Wow, I am getting paid to do this, it's such a fun thing for me." Then there are times when I have writer's block and I just can't write at all and I have a complete lack of faith in my writing. Sometimes there are weeks when I just dread writing.

As you can see, David is using standard Deepening Questions with Heidi. He is also digging into what she's passionate about at a deeper level. Since he knows she's a writer he is asking himself what could be moments in her life where writing feels the best. He then asks her what it's like when writing seems to flow, and he asks her to describe those feelings to him.

Asking a woman "What are you most passionate about?" is a classic Deepening Question. It's one of those phrases you can use over and over in Deepening. Whenever you can find a way to use that question, you'll bring the conversation to a deeper level and built more intimacy.

One lesson to learn from this example is to avoid going into negative spaces with a woman, as we saw in the previous chapter. Heidi began talking about writer's block, which is really a bad feeling. Instead of talking more about writer's block and trying to console her, David simply redirected her attention. It's utter suicide to try to fix a woman's problems. Our suggestion is to redirect her attention.

When Bob the bad seducer is with a woman and she mentions a problem he immediately asks her to describe the problem in great detail: "Oh, writer's block sounds terrible. Tell me more about it. Wow, that sounds like absolute torture. How often does it happen to you? I heard about a writer who had writer's block and she had to be put into a psych ward—do you think that would ever happen to you?" Bob stupidly thinks that if he acts sympathetically enough and allows a woman to share her deepest pain with him then she will like him. Bob in fact alienates women by asking so many serious and intense questions that he comes across as a complete downer. By asking women to describe their pain in greater detail Bob shoots himself in the foot and digs himself deeper into a hole that he can't get out of.

Rather than have Heidi talk about what's not working in her life or how often she has writer's block, David changes the subject and asks her what else she likes to write about and if she writes poetry. When he asks her questions about what she likes in her life he shows that he's interested in her, but he's not giving energy to the depressing things she's talking about. He is responding by guiding the conversation into a positive direction. Your job is to guide conversations into romantic and intimate spaces and avoid topics where a woman is likely to get depressed or feel pain.

DAVID: What gives you the most joy in writing?

Heidi: I like to go to coffee shops and observe people. I love to eavesdrop on people. It's fun for me to just start writing about the person I'm observing and imagine that I know them. I start writing dialog and imagining that I know what they're thinking. Sometimes my coffee-shop writing turns into short stories. It's really fun for me to do that kind of writing, it's just something silly I enjoy.

DAVID: That's interesting, Heidi. I don't get to meet a lot of women who are that creative. It's fun to hear about your writing.

HEIDI: Thanks, I love that kind of writing. I really enjoy observing people and learn a lot from watching people.

DAVID: Are you observing me right now?

HEIDI: No, not at all.

DAVID: Now I'm scared. [Jokingly]

HEIDI: I write some poetry but I've never had any published. I don't usually share my poetry with people; it's just a private thing.

DAVID: Maybe if we get to know each other better a time will come when you will want to share some poetry with me. I understand maybe now is not the right time to share it.

HEIDI: Do you write poetry?

DAVID: No I don't. I am more of a nonfiction writer, but I know what it's like to be in the flow like you were talking about earlier. Where you feel like the words are just flowing through you and it feels like you're in the dance of writing. Those are moments when you feel like you reach beyond what you're normally able to reach and you come up with material that is better than who you know yourself to be.

HEIDI: Yes, I know that feeling very well.

DAVID: An important part of my life is having work situations and friends in my life that bring out the better me and help me see myself in a new, better light. Having those people around makes life more fun and exciting.

HEIDI: I really like writing and you just made me think about how cool it is to be able to write something and allow someone else to see something briefly through your eyes and just know what it is like to be you just for a second.

RON: Let's interrupt for a second and examine David's conversation with Heidi. The conversation started off playful and easy and now it's getting much more intimate and intense. David's doing a good job having a heart-to-heart talk with Heidi.

DAVID: I started out that section affirming her. I told her I don't get to meet a lot of women who are as creative as she is.

RON: But you are also joking around, making some funny comments. You're teasing her, and that seems to be a good way to go with Heidi. She seems receptive to you and wouldn't be revealing so much about herself unless she felt comfortable with you.

DAVID: Humor is part of the bonding process. When Heidi tells me that she likes to observe people, I say, "Are you observing me?" I also said, "Maybe if we get to know each other better a time will come when you will want to share some poetry with me." I didn't push her real hard to show me her poetry; I just wanted to bring up the topic of going out with me in a fun, half-joking way.

One thing to notice is that Ron and I use a lot of "you" statements. In the most evocative visualizations, the person talking does his best to include the listener in the situation he is describing. For example, "You see yourself walking down the stairs"; "You see the things around you"; "You feel this." All of these examples use "you" to create clearer images. It's very useful to describe things from a "you" point of view. Talking to women is all about getting them to feel things, visualize things and imagine things.

That's why utilizing the you perspective in your speaking is so important. If you are describing how great it feels to be in the flow of writing you might say, "I feel so good when I am there and the energy is just flowing through me and the words are just flowing through me." It's a lot more powerful to say, "It feels so good when you are there and you are writing and the words are just flowing through you and you feel so connected to something larger than yourself, do you know what I mean?" I was just describing that feeling as if she is having it. My hope is that when I use you statements she'll say to herself, "It's amazing that I am with this guy who understands that."

RON: I want to point out that in the previous conversation Heidi is talking more then David. David is shutting up long enough to listen to what she's saying. He's then taking his time to construct a response that is either a bonding visualization or a question that pulls the conversation into a more intimate space.

Earlier in this book we talked about the power of describing romantic scenes and situations to women. We told you that what you describe to a woman is what she will feel. When you describe romantic scenes a woman has to go inside herself and experience those feelings. A new way to apply the principle of describing feelings is to ask a woman Romantic Questions. When a woman answers Romantic Questions and describes a romantic situation to you, she'll experience it while describing it to you. For example, if you ask a woman about her dream vacation and she describes it to you, she will have to go into her imagination and experience it. Whether you describe romantic scenes to a woman or you ask Romantic Questions that invoke a romantic response from a woman the result is the same: she experiences romantic feelings.

Let's go back are read more of the conversation.

DAVID: I would like to know more about you. Maybe I could read some of your writing sometime. What would it be like if we got together for a cup of coffee sometime and just talked more about writing and got to know each other a little better?

HEIDI: That would be great. I'd really enjoy that.

DAVID: I tell you what, give me your email address or phone number and we can set that up.

HEIDI: Sure, that sounds great.

Deepening Conversation 9

RON: Hi Katie, great to see you.

KATIE: You too, how are you?

RON: I'm doing great today. Your ring caught my attention. It looks really interesting, what's the story behind it?

KATIE: Well, actually, I got it when I was traveling. I was backpacking through Bangladesh and there was someone selling jewelry and this ring is actually a Celtic symbol. It looked really cool so I bought it.

RON: Bangladesh, what were you doing in Bangladesh?

DAVID: I want to point out that Ron effectively used the question "What's the story behind that?" to open up the conversation with Katie and then proceeded into Deepening Questions. This shows how "What's the story behind that?" can naturally lead into Deepening Conversations and then Romantic Conversations. We want you to keep an eye on how all the conversational modes you're learning in this book all fit together.

RON: What made you decide to go to Bangladesh? What did you do there?

KATIE: I just wanted to visit a place far away in a totally different culture. I wanted to go on a challenging journey that was different from my normal life.

RON: Wow, that is really brave, Katie.

KATIE: It was really fun and exciting. It was one of the most intense trips of my life.

RON: I don't get to meet women very often who have taken on life at that kind of level. It's really cool that you went there. How long were you in Bangladesh?

KATIE: I was there for about three months.

RON: Wow, three months in Bangladesh? That's a long time. You also said that you have a Celtic ring?

KATIE: It's a Celtic symbol of an eternal knot.

RON: An eternal knot? Let me see that for a second. [He reaches over and touches the ring] This is a cool ring. Where else do you like to travel?

DAVID: Let's jump in for a second. When you're talking to a woman it's helpful to be on the lookout for openings to touch her hand or her jewelry. Touching a woman in non-intrusive ways is great in building up to asking for a date. Ron seizes the opportunity to make things more physical with Katie by touching her ring.

RON: I mentioned that I thought Katie was brave for going to Bangladesh. This compliment was a way to validate her life. Another example of validating her is when I said I don't get to meet many women who have lived like that. An important aspect of Deepening is asking questions to find out what a woman values. From there, the next step is admiring what she values and feeding it back to her.

KATIE: Do you like to travel?

RON: Yes I do, although I rarely go places as unusual as Bangladesh. It's amazing when you travel, you get to see new things and experience a new culture. When you travel you get to let different parts of yourself come out. Do you know what I mean?

KATIE: Yes, that's one of the main reasons I love to see new places.

RON: I would be interested to know what part of your trip touched your heart the most.

KATIE: The way people were welcoming to me and let me into their homes. It is not something that you see every day. My favorite part of the trip was meeting new people. I made a lot of special connections.

RON: Did you have any experiences that kind of just sticks in your heart? Do you recall experiences that are postcard moments that you'll remember for the rest of your life? I'd be curious to know if you had experiences and moments like that.

DAVID: Let's jump in. What's interesting to me in this conversation is that Ron is taking this seemingly mundane conversation that has nothing romantic in it and progressively taking it to deeper levels of rapport building. Ron and Katie have a connection building. She is starting to trust him, and he is listening and feeding back the positive things she is saying. By listening and feeding back what he hears, Ron is showing his interest in Katie.

RON: Katie started asking me questions. But opening conversations with women are more about how you make them feel, not about your showing off, so I tried to avoid talking about myself and instead focused on feeding back to Katie the positive feelings of traveling.

Next, I asked additional Deepening Questions to get her talking more about traveling. I asked Katie, "When you are traveling, what touches your heart the most?" Then I asked her, "What are the post card moments that you will remember the most of your life?" These are Deepening Questions you might want to use when you talk to women.

KATIE: Well, it's not something I care to think about often, but there was a really bad storm and there was a mudslide that we somehow escaped. That part of the trip sticks out in my mind.

RON: Was there a good part to that crisis? Like feeling that you have a deeper appreciation for life? What was the most positive thing you walked away from that experience feeling?

DAVID: Let's jump in again. We've seen conversations move into negative directions before. We told you that it's important to redirect conversations into more positive topics. When Katie mentioned she was stuck in a mudslide the conversation could have become depressing and unpleasant. Ron was able to gently move the conversation to a different topic and keep focused on building his rapport with Katie.

RON: I noticed that Katie was running the horrible scene of barely escaping a mudslide in through mind. I didn't want her to feel the bad feelings associated with that experience, so I took the conversation in a different direction. I wasn't sure what to say to her, but I came back with, "Was there a good part to that crisis?" I knew I had to move quickly and come up with something to guide the conversation onto a different topic.

DAVID: If you had let Katie keep talking about the mudslide it could have become a depressing. She might have said, "Kids died in that mudslide..." So it's great that Ron interrupted her. Women don't always talk about upbeat subjects so you need to learn how to turn negative topics into positive ones.

You can handle negative topics by asking any of the following questions:

- "What was the best part of it?"

- "Was there a positive part in all of it?"

- "What did you learn from that experience?"

- "How has that experience changed you?"

KATIE: Surviving the mudslide made me appreciate life a lot more. At the same time I felt proud of myself for surviving such a scary experience and challenging myself. I really like pushing myself and putting myself out there. I'm glad I had such an intense experience in Bangladesh.

RON: I can see in talking with you that you really push yourself and live life on the edge. It seems like you're someone who is strong in the face of uncertainty. I really admire how you live life fully.

RON: One thing I noticed in talking to Katie is that she pushes herself to try new things and is really courageous and adventurous. In Deepening I am looking for what she is passionate about and what she values, so I wanted to let her know that I see her as a gutsy woman. I also complimented in a way that was deeply personal and intimate. Let's look at some more.

RON: I know exactly how it feels to really push yourself and really go after what you want. Like when you meet someone you can connect with or you feel like they open their heart to you in a certain way. There is something really special about being open like that. I don't think we get enough of those moments in our lives.

KATIE: Being in Bangladesh and having people be so kind to me made me want to be more open to people in my everyday life. I try to be friendly when I am out at the grocery store doing little tasks and errands that seem mundane.

RON: It's been great to meet you, but I need to run in a second. Maybe we could get together for a cup of coffee sometime and talk some more.

Katie: Sure, that would be great. Maybe you could tell me about your travel experiences.

RON: What is your phone number and email address? It would be great to go out sometime this week.

KATIE: Here, I'll write down my number and email.

RON: When Katie mentioned that she tries to be friendly when she's out shopping and running errands, I thought that was a good segue to asking her out. I wanted to end the conversation on a high point. I thought that if she wasn't willing to go out with me after talking for so long it was unlikely that she'd give me her number if we talked any longer.

Here's a good phrase to use when asking a woman for her number: "It's been nice talking to you, perhaps we can get together sometime and talk about this some more." You don't need anything fancy or special. You don't need a perfect line, you just need to open your mouth and ask her out. After you have her phone number or email address you can set up the coffee date.

more on Deepening

Let's recap what we've learned in this chapter:

Conversations with women sometimes fail. Deepening Conversations don't always go well. There is no magical formula to have successful conversations with women 100 percent of the time. Sometimes the conversation goes well and sometimes you flat on your face.

When bad-luck seducer Bob has Deepening Conversations that go poorly, he's shocked. "I did what Louis & Copeland said in that damn book and the one woman I talked to didn't want to make out with me. Those guys are jerks. I want my money back!" Bob fails to realize that most conversations with women will not lead to getting a phone number, let alone sex. Bob's so focused on finding a magical solution to getting women to date him that he forgets that talking to women is a numbers game, and work. Instead of talking to several women until one is interested in talking to him, Bob would rather blame everyone else and complain.

The trick in talking to women is to be persistent. When one conversation goes poorly, move on and talk to another woman. When a conversation goes poorly, just chalk it up to experience. If you are persistent and talk to dozens of women, you'll eventually have successful Deepening Conversations. After a few successful Deepening Conversations you'll get a phone number and things will keep progressing from there. If you are willing to do the work and be patient, success is inevitable.

Include yourself when describing scenes. In Deepening you are creating romantic images through descriptions of romantic scenes. In Advanced Deepening you are describing scenes where you and your conversational partner are together in the scene.

For instance, instead of describing a great concert, describe a situation where you and she are at a concert together having a wonderful time. When you describe romantic scenes with the two of you, a woman will have to go inside and imagine that picture of the two of you together. By describing scenes to a woman you increase your chances of getting her number. You'll also improve your chances of having her see you as a romantic possibility.

We realize that including yourself when describing scenes to women can be confusing. It's a new skill that you need to practice. Try writing out potential conversations and practice asking questions out loud at home. The more practice you have the easier it will be to include yourself in scenes when you have a woman in front of you.

Assume rapport. By this we mean that when you're talking to a woman you should assume she is enjoying talking to you and being with you. When a salesman assumes rapport, he assumes that his prospective customer likes him, is interested in what he's selling, has similar values and trusts him. It's crucial to assume the best when you're with a woman.

Bob assumes that every woman he talks to will hate him and that every interaction will go poorly. When he talks to women and asks Deepening Questions his certainty that the interaction will go poorly comes across in his tone of voice and his presence. Because Bob is so certain his conversations will go poorly, he comes across as angry and mean.

You can teach yourself to assume rapport by reminding yourself that women are interested in talking to you and find you attractive. You can tell yourself that the interaction is going well. When you assume women like you, you will not only feel more confident and more relaxed, you will also be more romantic, easygoing and likeable. Assuming rapport is crucial in talking to women.

Ask open-ended questions. We've mentioned the importance of asking open-ended questions before. You need to cast the widest net possible when talking to women. The goal is to create a space for women to feel comfortable and relaxed talking to you. Bob is a master of asking questions so that women feel trapped. Here's an example of Bob's attempt at Deepening:

BOB: Hi, did you see the new John Travolta movie?

WOMAN: No, I haven't. Did you?

BOB: So you didn't see that movie? Why not? Is it because you don't
like movies or is it because you don't like John Travolta?

WOMAN: Oh, I just haven't seen a movie in few months. I've been
working a lot. Did you see the movie?

BOB: Oh, so you must really hate your job since you have to work so
much. I hate jobs where they force you to work overtime and don't
pay you.

WOMAN: Oh, I must go now. Bye.

Bob asks closed ("yes-or-no") questions that have an accusatory feel to
them rather than open-ended questions that encourage a woman to talk.
Bob not only asks yes-or-no questions, he argues with the woman's
response rather than encouraging her to talk. Don't box women into
answering yes-or-no questions or questions that limit their options. Ask
open-ended questions so that larger conversations can develop.

Fun, fun, fun. What's more romantic to a woman, a man who is
stressed, nervous and uptight or someone who is relaxed, playful and
having fun? The answer is clear: men who are able to enjoy themselves
are much more attractive than guys who are uptight and worried.

Women's bullshit detectors are much more attuned than are men's.
Women know when you're not interested in talking to them, when you're
nervous and when you're not having fun. So we strongly recommend
you find fun ways to make conversations with women fun. Bring up topics that are enjoyable for you. Mention things you find funny. Ask ques-

tions you're curious about. Have a good time.

Talking to women should not be an ordeal. When Bob talks to women he's constantly preoccupied with asking the perfect question. He is so caught up with his own thoughts and concerns that talking to a woman is a stressful, horrible affair. Bob is too afraid to take any risks and so he falls deeper into a fear spiral. He is too afraid to share anything about himself, mention anything he considers funny or ask any questions that are romantic. His fear creates a situation that is unpleasant for both himself and the woman.

Here are some surefire ways to *not* have fun when you're with a woman:

- Trying to be perfect

- Asking questions that you don't care anything about

- Never sharing anything about yourself

- Not taking any romantic risks

- Worrying that you're doing everything wrong

- Never smiling

- Solely focusing on getting into her pants

- Never cracking jokes

- Worrying that everything you say will offend her

- Solely focusing on having her not think you're trying to get into her pants

If you are able to let go, have fun and take some risks with women, you'll be more relaxed and more fun to be around. Fun attracts more fun; fear tends to create more fear.

Don't be a stranger. When talking to women be on the lookout for details she's sharing with you she wouldn't normally share with a stranger. These are details you want to acknowledge.

Deepening Conversations are all about creating a connection with a woman that makes her feel that you see something in her to which most people are not privy. When you are able to see things in her that most men don't see, intimacy is created. When you start creating emotional connections, she'll want to connect more deeply with you.

Admire her. You want to be the kind of guy who acknowledges women. Everyone feels good when they're acknowledged. When you admire a woman for her strengths or take notice of what is special to her and what is special about her, she'll feel closer to you.

Ask about great moments in her life. In Deepening you are focusing on a woman's life and looking for special moments to acknowledge. You are looking for times in her life when she felt best, moments she's most proud of, her accomplishments and her passions. Ask women about great moments in their past and great moments in their current life. Two great questions to use are "What are you most passionate about?" and "What are the postcard moments that you will remember for the rest of your life?"

Don't push too hard. You do not need to push women into sexual or romantic talk. The purpose of Deepening is often just to bond. Without the foundation of bonding there is no hope of turning things sexual. If you skip this early work you'll fail miserably later on. The goal of Deepening is to create a bond, develop rapport and lay the groundwork for asking for a number. Sometimes the conversation turns romantic; other times it's much lighter. In either case the goal is to move from being a stranger to creating enough of a connection to take the next step.

Some women are weird, wacky and strange. We all encounter women who say unusual things. If she's worth pursuing, stop focusing on the unusual aspects of her personality. Once you are in a relationship, you need to ignore the aspects of a woman's personality that bother you. It's called coping with the harsh reality.

The importance of "you" statements. The most evocative writing and visualizations strive to put the listener in the scene by using the word "you." It's very useful to describe things from a "you" point of view, ie, "Yea, I think it's so great when you are having a perfect day, and you can just breathe in and really feel good about what you've accomplished."

Talking to women is all about getting them to feel things, visualize things and imagine things. That's why using the "you" perspective in your speaking is so important. Taking on a "you" perspective might take some practice, but it's worth it. Do you understand?

Women might turn the tables on you. Eventually a woman will turn the tables on you and start asking questions about your life and passions. We recommend you reply with romantic and open-ended responses. You need to reveal details about yourself, but you can do so in a way that is not bragging or time-consuming or boring for the woman.

When a woman asks Bob what he's passionate about in his life he begins talking to her about his new flat-panel computer screen, the great screen resolution it has, and how the competitor's version sucks. Bob goes off on a 10-minute tangent on a topic the woman could care less about.

Bad move. Just give a short response about yourself and then ask additional Deepening Questions and refocus the conversation on her.

Shut up and listen. When you're conducting Deepening Conversations it's crucial that she talks more than you do. When you're having a Deepening Conversation, shut your pie hole while she answers your question. Don't interrupt a woman when she's talking. Instead, listen and take time to construct a response that is either a visualization based on what she's just told you or a question that evokes more information from her.

When Bob conducts Deepening Conversations, he never shuts up. He interrupts the woman when she's talking about her favorite vacation and brags about his Alaskan cruise. Bob constantly interrupts women when they're telling him key information. Rather than listen, Bob enjoys offering his opinions on what a woman is telling him. When Jennifer told him about the best parts of her job, he lectured her on why she should quit her job and find a higher-paying profession.

Bob can't contain his thoughts enough to create a bond with women. You need to shut up long enough for them to respond. A good rule of thumb is they should talk 70 percent of the time, you should talk 30 percent of the time.

Talking to women is like fishing. If the first question you ask a woman doesn't elicit a juicy response, move on to another question. In Deepening you are fishing by asking questions and finding out what she's passionate about. Once you get a strong response from her, ask more questions and feed back more situations to her. Just like with fishing, you're patiently waiting for a bite. Once you get one, you quickly go for it and get her talking about what she's passionate about.

Deepening Conversations can lead to touching and more. When you can touch a woman as part of a Deepening Conversation you are helping escalate the seduction. Most men wait until the end of a date before doing anything physical. During Deepening Conversations, however, there are often openings for touch. When asking a woman about her ring, for example, you could touch her hand. When sitting next to a woman, you could "accidentally" brush against her arm.

When you touch a woman, do so gently and as unobtrusively as possible. If a woman reacts negatively, that is a sign to slow the seduction down. If a woman seems open to touching, it's a sign to go for the next level of touching or kissing.

When the conversation goes downhill. Several times during this chapter we mentioned how important it is to avoid talking about depressing topics. When a woman starts talking about bad experiences or depressing topics, your job is to redirect the conversation to a different topic. Here are a few phrases you can use:

- "What was the best part of it?"

- "Was there a good part to that crisis?"

- "Did you have a deeper appreciation for life?"

- "What was the most positive thing you walked away from that experience feeling?"

CONCLUSION

Hopefully, you are starting to get a feel for how all of this can fit together. You initiate with women by saying hi, using the goodbye introduction, or though any other social means that gets you talking to another human being. From there you take some deeper risks, doing the flirting moves to get yourself out of the "friends" zone, asking "What's the story behind that?", using situational flirting, and, now, adding in Deepening conversations.

Now we'll move on to the next step in talking to women: Asking Romantic Questions. •

CHAPTER 10
Romantic Questions, Part 1

We've talked about the importance of interrupting and initiating, the Hi Program, the Goodbye Introduction, "What's the story behind that?", Situational Flirting, and Deepening. Practicing each of these conversational tools will give you the power you need to initiate with women, to interrupt them on deeper and deeper levels, and to redirect their thoughts—and possibly their romantic attention—to you.

Now you're ready to add another skill to the mix: asking Romantic Questions. Romantic Questions build on the tools you already have to take your conversations with women to an even deeper and more seductive level.

Before we can get into asking Romantic Questions, though, it's important for you to review the power of description, because description is the key that makes Romantic Questions work.

What You Describe Is What She Feels

There is a fundamental concept that underlies everything romantic that you say to a woman. It is an idea about the way people's brains work, and it is very simple: when you describe something to somebody, she must go inside and imagine it or experience it so she can understand what you are talking about.

The classic example of this phenomenon involves describing an elephant. It is huge, it has big white tusks, gray skin, a long trunk and big floppy ears. In order to understand this description, you had to imagine what we were describing, at least to some extent. Even if you wanted to resist us and decided that, no matter what, you were not going to imagine an elephant, you'd still have to imagine one to know what you shouldn't imagine. This is a basic principle of how the mind works: if you describe something to someone, they automatically imagine it.

This little quirk in the human mind really works in your favor when you talk to women because it doesn't only work if you describe things like elephants. It also works if you describe experiences like love, romance, seduction and arousal. If we were to describe an experience to you, you'd have to imagine having that experience, at least to some small extent, simply to understand what we were talking about. (The extent to which you had that experience would depend on how well we described it.) It's an involuntary reaction, and everyone has it.

This is your access into the emotional being of a woman. If you are talking to a woman and describing romantic experiences, erotic experiences or emotional experiences, she is going to have to go into her mind and experience those experiences just to track with the conversation. When a woman has those feelings while she is looking at you then you are having a romantic interaction.

If you don't believe that describing an experience can influence feelings, look at it from the other side: no one would disagree that describing disgusting things has an effect on someone's internal emotional state. You don't want your dinner companion to describe creepy, slimy worms while you're eating spaghetti because you'd naturally imagine worms and feel revolted by the plate of spaghetti in front of you. This mirrors the basic principle of seductive conversation.

DAVID: Just last night I was doing some Internet flirting. I was asking a woman about romantic experiences she had had and out of the blue she started into this tirade about abortion and how bad abortion is and how she is totally against it. Now one thing I could have done was fight with her about it, but already she was imaging all this horrible stuff about abortion in her head and feeling her feelings about it. Fighting would only have made it worse. I could also have asked her not to think about it, but she still would have had to imagine what she shouldn't be thinking about, so it might have made those horrible pictures she was imagining even more vivid.

So I let her say what she had to say and then I came back with "Let's talk more about dating. Let's talk more about romantic experiences. Let's talk about how the heart opens up with someone who you really feel connected to." Those were the kind of experiences I wanted us to be talking about so she would be having those romantic experiences inside and connect them to me, rather than having her think about abortion and connecting that to me. And it worked; she got off her abortion tirade and we had a great romantic talk.

You have probably been in an experience with a woman when it seemed like everything just went sour. You were getting along great, then suddenly there was a problem and you couldn't seem to fix it no matter what you did. If you were to look at a transcript of that conversation, you'd probably find that the conversation took a turn into something like rape, child abuse, abortion or something else that she found really unpleasant. Her mind became filled with unpleasant pictures while she was interacting with you and before you knew it, the romantic vibe was gone.

You might even have caused the problem. Perhaps you talked about things you didn't even realize you were talking about; perhaps you talked about porn or war or something else that, when she imagined it, really turned her off. Sometimes it can be a lot subtler than you realize. With women, you really don't know what is going to happen; you have to stay awake, be present and pay attention to the conversational topics that turn her on and the things that turn her off.

We will get into the specifics of using romantic descriptions with women, but here's the bottom line about how we use them: through talking, questioning and listening, we look for things that women are passionate about and value. We then either get women to describe the feelings of those passions and values to us or we describe them to the women. They are then able to experience and dwell on those feelings while being with us. This creates a very real and romantic connection.

Success with women isn't totally about what you look like, what you do or how much money you make, even though those things are obviously factors. Success with women is about how you make women feel—that's what's most important. If you make a woman feel excited, turned on and appreciated, she's going to be a lot more likely to go for you.

In the next few chapters you will learn the specific flirting skills necessary to turn anything that a woman says into a Romantic Conversation. We mean it—if she tells you she's an accountant, you'll be able to turn that into a Romantic Conversation. The first step is understanding the structure of Romantic Questions.

THE STRUCTURE OF ROMANTIC QUESTIONS

A properly asked Romantic Question has three components:

- The excuse

- The description

- The question

Let's look at each part.

THE EXCUSE. When you ask a woman a Romantic Question, you need to start with an excuse. The excuse answers the question the woman will be asking herself about your question, which is "Why is he asking me this?" If you can answer that question right away with your excuse, it will be much easier for her to open up to you.

Most of the time, women you don't know well are going to ask themselves some combination of their safety questions when you first interrupt them or when you take the conversation into deeper, riskier territory. Remember, these questions are "What is he going to do to me?," "How long will it take?" and "Why is he saying this to me?"

When you ask a Romantic Question, the excuse answers the question "Why is he saying this to me?" It gives her a context for what you're asking, which helps a woman relax into the interaction.

A Romantic Question standing on its own can seem invasive and scary, but when you add an excuse and description, almost any question can become palatable.

Let's try this out on one of the tackiest questions you can ask a woman: "Do you believe in love at first sight?" You'll probably agree with us that most women would think of this as a hackneyed line, which it is. But let's see what happens when we add an excuse to it. Which question do you think would make it easier for a woman to relax and answer: "Hey, do you believe in love at first sight?" or "I've been talking to my friends about this and sort of taking an informal survey. Do you think people can fall in love at first sight?"

We aren't recommending such an overused line, but the second version of this question would be easier for a woman to answer. That's because it has an excuse attached to it. The woman can say to herself, "Oh, he's asking me this because he's been talking about it to his friends. Okay."

THE DESCRIPTION. This part of a Romantic Question helps guide the woman to the kind of answer you are looking for. It also describes the kind of feelings you want her to imagine having while she is answering the question.

Let's add a description to our test question: "I've been talking to my friends about this and sort of taking an informal survey. It seems like sometimes you meet someone and there's just an immediate click, do you know what I mean? Like, 'Oh, it's you,' even though you've never met before. So I've been wondering, do you think people can fall in love at first sight?"

The description we added to this Romantic Question suggests the feeling you want your conversational partner to feel and also guides her toward the kind of answer you are looking for. Again, it's worth noting that even a tacky question can start seeming downright interesting when you add an excuse and description to it.

THE QUESTION. The question is simply the Romantic Question itself— in our example, "Do you think people can fall in love at first sight?" Once again, let's look at the Romantic Question in its entirety. Notice how much more normal-sounding and less tacky the question is when the excuse and description are in place. Then think about how well this would work with a question that hasn't already been beaten to death in every bar in western civilization:

"I've been talking to my friends about this and sort of taking an informal survey. It seems like sometimes you meet someone and there's just an immediate click, do you know what I mean? Like, 'Oh, it's you,' even though you've never met before. So I've been wondering, do you think people can fall in love at first sight?"

Romantic Questions push the conversation into a romantic direction. When you ask a Romantic Question, you are taking things to a more intimate level. You need to be respectful of that fact, by setting up your questions in the most non-invasive way that you can. The way you do that is by having an excuse and a description before you ask your Romantic Question.

Let's look at some examples.

Example 1

THE ROMANTIC QUESTION: "What makes your heart flutter?"

You don't just ask that question outright because it would sound awkward and weird. You'd dump her right into her safety questions: "Why is he saying this to me? What's he going to do to me?" You need to set up your question with our three-step process.

Here's the full way of asking it: "I was thinking the other day about how amazing it is to be moved to the point where your heart flutters. Maybe you've seen a piece of artwork or heard some music and it's like the passion just builds in you and you feel it so intensely in your heart. I'd be curious to know, what makes your heart flutter? What's an example in your life of that?"

Let's break that example down into the excuse, the description and the question itself:

THE EXCUSE. "I was thinking the other day about how amazing it is to be moved to the point where your heart flutters." That answers the question "Why is he asking me this?" You were thinking about it the other day, that's why you're asking about it.

THE DESCRIPTION. "It's like the passion just builds in you and you feel it so intensely in your heart." You describe what you want her to experience so she has to go inside and experience that description, at least a little bit. This also guides her into the kind of answer you're looking for.

THE QUESTION. "I'd be curious to know, what makes your heart flutter? What's an example in your life of that?" Now she knows why you asked, she's felt the feeling a little bit and she's more likely to give you the kind of emotional, romantic answer you're looking for.

EXAMPLE 2

THE ROMANTIC QUESTION: "Have you ever met someone and felt like you were meeting them again for the first time?"

Once again, you wouldn't just dump this question on someone without preparation.

You might say: "I was talking to some friends the other night over dinner and we were talking about the feeling of when you meet someone and feel like you've known them before. One person was really into the past-life thing, and I wasn't sure what to think about that. I've certainly had those experiences where you meet someone and you look at them and you feel like you've known them before. It's like you're meeting them again, rather than for the first time. Do you know what I mean? So, I'd be curious to know, if you'd be willing to share about it, have you ever met someone and felt like you've met them before?"

Let's break it apart:

THE EXCUSE. "I was talking to some friends the other night over dinner and we were talking about the feeling of when you meet someone and feel like you've known them before." You were talking about it with friends the other night, so there's a reason it's on your mind.

THE DESCRIPTION. "One person was really into the past-life thing, and I wasn't sure what to think about that. I've certainly had those experiences where you meet someone and you look at them and you feel like you've known them before. It's like you're meeting them again, rather than for the first time." This description is great because it runs a little visualization on her and really paints a word picture of the kind of feeling you want her to experience as she looks at you. It will also guide her in selecting the kind of answer you're looking for.

THE QUESTION. "Have you ever met someone and felt like you've met them before?" When you put it this way it doesn't sound like a corny pickup line, which it would if you asked it straight out. Asking in this way gives her the opportunity to share about herself and her experiences of feeling a real connection when first meeting someone—and to look at you while she describes, and feels, those feelings.

Example 3

THE ROMANTIC QUESTION: "What was it like the first time you had a crush on someone?"

This question asked by itself sounds ridiculous.

But let's add an excuse and description and see how it sounds: "I was talking to a buddy from high school who I hadn't seen in a long time. We were looking back on high school and talking about first loves and crushes and how fun and exciting it was. It was this new, tender and exciting feeling of being so excited and turned on and really into someone, you know? I wonder if you can recall the first time you realized you had a crush on someone. What was that like for you?"

Let's break it down to the three parts:

THE EXCUSE. "I was talking to a buddy from high school who I hadn't seen in a long time. We were looking back on high school and talking about first loves and crushes and how fun and exciting it was."

THE DESCRIPTION. "It was this new, tender and exciting feeling of being so excited and turned on and really into someone, you know?"

THE QUESTION. "I wonder if you can recall the first time you realized you had a crush on someone. What was that like for you?"

Example 4

THE ROMANTIC QUESTION: "What's a special place you enjoy going to for vacation that makes you feel really good and really alive?"

Obviously, you would not want to just throw that at a woman.

You might say: "I was watching TV the other night and I saw an ad for traveling to Jamaica. And I thought, 'Gosh, that sounds like a really great time.' I've never been there. It looked so great. The clear water, being able to see the fish under the water in a glass-bottom boat or going snorkeling and having an incredible vacation. It got me thinking and asking people about their ideal vacation. So I'd be curious to know, if you'd be willing to share, what's your ideal vacation? It can be one you've been on or maybe one you'd like to go on. I'd just be curious to know."

Let's break it down:

THE EXCUSE. "I was watching TV the other night and I saw an ad for traveling to Jamaica. And I thought, 'Gosh, that sounds like a really great time.'"

THE DESCRIPTION. "I've never been there. It looked so great. The clear water, being able to see the fish under the water in a glass-bottom boat or going snorkeling and having an incredible vacation. It got me thinking and asking people about their ideal vacation."

THE QUESTION. "So I'd be curious to know, if you'd be willing to share, what's your ideal vacation? It can be one you've been on or maybe one you'd like to go on. I'd just be curious to know."

Example 5

THE ROMANTIC QUESTION: "What's your favorite moment in a kiss?"

If you asked a woman what her favorite moment is in a kiss flat out you'd come across as a real freak-boy.

Try this instead: "I was talking to my friend Tanya the other day and we were talking about kissing. We were talking about the magic of kissing and the magical moments that occur during a kiss. There is a moment when you close your eyes. There's the moment when your lips first touch. There is a moment when your tongues first entwine. It's all so amazing. I'd be curious to know, what's your favorite moment in a kiss?"

This is obviously a more intense question than the others. You are bringing up something very intimate and describing something that can lead directly to sex.

But this is a good thing. If you've been doing the other flirting moves, she's already thinking of you as a possible romantic partner, and it's appropriate to heat things up a bit. This is a great way to do that. At the right moment, this question could really work for you. You might add in a whisper or get closer to her ear. It might turn into a very sensual moment. This might even turn into a kiss.

Here are the three parts:

THE EXCUSE. "I was talking to my friend Tanya the other day and we were talking about kissing. We were talking about the magic of kissing and the magical moments that occur during a kiss."

THE DESCRIPTION. "There is a moment when you close your eyes. There's the moment when your lips first touch. There is a moment when your tongues first entwine. It's all so amazing."

THE QUESTION. "I'd be curious to know, what's your favorite moment in a kiss?"

Example 6

THE ROMANTIC QUESTION: "What are some of your favorite romantic movies?"

Most guys are not particularly into romantic movies, but it's good to ask a woman about them because her answer to this question can tell you a lot about how she likes to be seduced. It'll provide information you will find useful on dates with her. It'll also get her describing and feeling some of her favorite romantic feelings, while looking at you.

So here's what you might ask: "I am usually into action films myself, but lately I've been looking at some more romantic films. Sometimes I see movies that have such a romantic feel to them. They have such sweet, strong romantic moments in them—a couple is being swept off their feet, falling deeply in love, like a Cary Grant-Audrey Hepburn sort of moment. I'd be curious to know, if you'd be willing to share, if you were going to recommend a romantic film to me, what would it be?"

The three parts:

THE EXCUSE. "I am usually into action films myself, but lately I've been looking at some more romantic films."

THE DESCRIPTION. "Sometimes I see movies that have such a romantic feel to them. They have such sweet, strong romantic moments in them—a couple is being swept off their feet, falling deeply in love, like a Cary Grant-Audrey Hepburn sort of moment."

THE QUESTION. "I'd be curious to know, if you'd be willing to share, if you were going to recommend a romantic film to me, what would it be?"

Example 7

THE ROMANTIC QUESTION: "What was your first kiss like?"

Put it this way: "I've been asking my friends this question lately and it really seems to generate some pretty interesting conversations. Everybody has a first-kiss story—that feeling of doing something so romantic for the first time can really be so incredibly moving. So I'm wondering, if you would care to share, what was your first kiss like?"

The three parts of this question:

THE EXCUSE. "I've been asking my friends this question lately and it really seems to generate some pretty interesting conversations."

THE DESCRIPTION. "Everybody has a first-kiss story—that feeling of doing something so romantic for the first time can really be so incredibly moving."

THE QUESTION. "So I'm wondering, if you would care to share, what was your first kiss like?"

Is this whole Romantic Question sequence starting to make sense to you? There's some subtlety to it, but it's not rocket science or brain surgery (or, as one of our students called it, "rocket surgery"). You are not just hitting on someone. You are developing a connection with her. You are creating a connection based on things she cares about, things she has passion about.

Common Questions About Romantic Questions

Here are some of the most common questions men have about using Romantic Questions.

QUESTION: How intimate should the questions be?

ANSWER: As you've no doubt noticed, the questions vary in intensity from relatively low-risk questions like "What's a special place you enjoy going to for vacation?" to relatively high-risk questions like "What's your favorite moment in a kiss?" As you learn to improvise these questions, you'll come up with ones that are even milder and others that are even riskier. You decide how intimate a question to ask by assessing two things: how things are going with the woman and the level of risk you want to take.

Most of the time, you'll want to start with the lower-risk questions, and, as that goes well, move up to the higher-risk questions. If you're feeling especially ballsy, you can move up to the higher-risk questions faster. If you ask them with a sense of certainty that everything is okay then things will probably go fine.

You can tell that you are risking too much if you find yourself leaving out the excuse and description parts of the Romantic Question. When guys get tense, they tend to leave out the excuse and the description and just go to the question. If that happens to you, you need to slow down, take some deep breaths and ask a lower-risk question.

Q: What should I do if she asks me the Romantic Question back?

A: This happens all the time, and you should be ready for it. For instance, if you ask a woman, "What is your idea of a really romantic date?" and she answers you and asks you the same question back, you need to answer her. Simply describe a date that sounds really romantic to you. There's no big trick to it; just talk about a situation that sounds romantic to you. If you can use your words to paint a picture for the two of you together, that's good. If your description is similar to her idea of a romantic date, even better.

Obviously, you will want to speak from the romancer part of your-self when you answer this question. If she describes her ideal romantic date as an evening by the seashore, just her and her lover eating lobster and drinking fine wine, you won't want to respond by telling her that your ideal romantic date is an evening drinking beer at the demolition derby followed by a night of hot sex with your favorite Penthouse centerfold. Get into the spirit of the thing and describe something romantic that she would also enjoy.

Q: Won't showing my romantic interest be embarrassing for us both?

A: It's true that if you use Romantic Questions properly she'll know you're interested in her romantically. However, because you're approaching the seduction in such a romantic, nonslimy way, she is very likely to think that your desire for her is a very good thing rather than a creepy thing she needs to get away from.

Asking Romantic Questions is also great because you can start with the less risky, less obvious ones and work your way up to the more intense ones. If she balks on the less risky ones and seems uncomfortable, you know not to go on to the more intense questions until you get better results with those less risky questions. In this way you can find out her level of interest step by step without risking making things really weird for you both by asking something too intense out of the blue.

Q: How often should I ask Romantic Questions during an interaction with a woman?

A: You'll see examples of how we use Romantic Questions in the dialogs that are coming up in this book, but the short answer is this: pepper them in. Romantic Questions are not the sole focus of your discussion. You talk about the weather, the news, you do some of the Flirting Moves, ask her about her job and throw in Romantic Questions. If you pepper them in, it will feel natural.

Asking too many Romantic Questions is not the problem most of our students have. The first problem most of our students have is not asking Romantic Questions at all. The second problem most of our students have is dropping out the excuse and the description and just asking the question part of the Romantic Question. The last and certainly the least problem our students have is asking too many Romantic Questions.

Having said that, it will probably feel awkward the first few times you ask one of these questions. As you practice, you may leave some interactions with women feeling as if you asked too many Romantic Questions or worrying that you overwhelmed her with them. That's okay; it's part of the learning process. Overdoing it once or twice is invaluable to your learning how to use Romantic Questions. And don't worry—it won't hurt her if you ask "too many" Romantic Questions. She's made of tougher stuff than that.

Q: How should I get started with Romantic Questions?

A: First, choose one or two Romantic Questions and learn them by heart. Remember, that means you have to learn all three parts of the question: the excuse, the description and the question itself.

Second, practice speaking the entire Romantic Question out loud. When you're alone at home or in your car or getting ready to go to work in the morning, speak your Romantic Questions. This gets your body used to saying the questions—which is of course what you are going to end up doing. When you are in front of a woman, it does you no good to be great at saying the Romantic Question silently in your own mind. You need to be able to speak the question, and that is why you practice it out loud.

Third, try it out with a woman. Perhaps you meet a woman at a coffee shop and you've said hi, done some of the Flirting Moves like smiling, holding eye contact and winking at her, all perhaps in the context of doing some Situational Flirting. Perhaps you've asked her "What's the story behind that?" about her necklace and that's generated some sharing conversations. Things are going well. Then ask your Romantic Question. Make your excuse, give your description and ask away. Voilà!

Q: Should I learn these questions by heart or improvise them on the spot?

A: At first you will want to learn one or two Romantic Questions by heart and try them out with women to see what kind of conversations and romantic feelings that they spark.

As you get more experience, you'll find that it's natural to improvise the questions or parts of the questions. At first you will probably find it is most natural to improvise new excuses and descriptions to go with the Romantic Questions you intend to ask. In time, you'll be able to improvise the questions too. As you relax more with a woman, you'll be able to get more curious about her and about her life. Your curiosity about her will guide you in spontaneously creating new Romantic Questions that are well-suited for her.

CONCLUSION

As we'll see in the next chapter, asking Romantic Questions leads naturally to asking her for her phone number and email address. Asking Romantic Questions naturally segues into both of you wanting to have a date. Asking Romantic Questions naturally segues into having a woman think of you in romantic terms. On your dates, you can ask Romantic Questions to deepen into the feelings of romance. Romantic Questions often lead to great opportunities for the first kiss.

You can ask Romantic Questions before the date, on the date and whenever you can get them in. You can ask Romantic Questions online, in a first meeting—anywhere. Romantic Questions are an important part of your seduction toolbox. The more familiar you are with this skill and the more comfortable you are with it, the more often you'll be able to use it to your advantage.

The cool part about asking Romantic Questions is that, once again, it's not about bamboozling, hypnotizing, tricking, or scamming on women. Romantic Questions are a way for you to authentically learn about a woman, to get into her world and to make a real connection. When you ask a Romantic Question, you give a woman a gift and in the process find out what kind of connection can exist between the two of you. •

CHapter 11
Romantic Questions, Part 2

Let's look at some real examples of Romantic Conversations with women. For each one of these examples we'll give you the dialog and break in occasionally with some play by play so you can know what was going on in our minds as we were conducting these conversations.

As you read these dialogs, remember: you are only getting the text of the conversations. You aren't getting the unspoken social cues that go along with them, so let's bring you up to speed: during all of these conversations we are smiling and our voices are friendly. Sometimes in these dialogs we may say things that would seem confrontational if they were said in an angry or harsh manner. But they're fine here because our manner is light and playful. For instance, at one point Ron says to a woman, "So you can relate to the women who was married, yet she was sleeping with somebody else?" As you'll see in the dialog below, the woman Ron was talking to didn't take what he said the wrong way. That was because he was smiling, they were having a good time together and it was clear to her that he was joking with her, not insulting her.

WHat Is It Like to Feel SpeCial?

In this example Ron is going to talk to Terri and ask her the Romantic Question "What is it like when you feel very special on a date?" Here it is:

RON: I was talking to some friends of mine last night about this and we were wondering. Sometimes it seems like a date is really going great, there's great flow and things seem to really be cooking and you feel incredibly special. So I was wondering: what is it like when you feel very special on a date?

TERRI: When I am the focus, when I am included in the conversation. I was just on a date last week and it was wonderful because the gentleman leaned forward on the table when he was talking to me and I knew there was interest. It was very clear.

RON: Okay, cool. So you are the kind of women who likes it when a guy takes charge of the conversation yet includes you?

TERRI: Oh yes, absolutely.

RON: So you want him to say things like "You look beautiful" or "You know I can't wait to," you know, or "I would love to kiss you"? That sort of thing?

TERRI: Yes, the attention and the openness. I want men who don't just question me but who are willing to share about themselves too.

Let's break in here and take a look at our story so far. Ron is really doing well with Terri. He got the question out and she is really giving him some information. As you read this you should be asking yourself: what is Terri revealing about herself that might help in the seduction? Ron has learned that she is really turned on by a guy leaning forward on the table, so he puts that data point into his mind and he'll use that later. He'll lean forward and show interest as soon as he can.

Let's look at some more of the conversation.

RON: Do you have any questions for me?

TERRI: Yes, why are you here?

RON: Why am I here on earth?

TERRI: I mean at this place at this time.

RON: To be with you. Why else would I be here?

TERRI: But we just met!

RON: Well, I believe that things happen for a reason. Don't you think that's true?

TERRI: Yes.

RON: So I think this was a good thing that we are meeting and talking, and I think maybe it was meant to be. So from where I am sitting, maybe we could talk again. I would love to call you and go out for coffee and just have the fun continue because I would hate for this to be a one-time thing.

TERRI: All right, do you want my number?

RON: Yes, would you like to write it on my hand or write it on my stomach?

TERRI: Well, I think you can memorize if you are really paying attention. [Laughs]

RON: I am, but perhaps I should write it down too, just to be sure.

Let's tear apart the second half of this interaction. She says she wants guys who will share about themselves, so he asks her "Do you have any questions for me?" to show her that he is open to sharing about himself.

She came back with a silly question, "What are you doing here?" Very often, when a woman does something like this, it's an invitation to be silly, an invitation to play together in some way. Ron picked up on that and was able to play with what she said. He made a joke and it went over well. He was willing to just open up his mouth and say whatever came out and have it be all right. Remember what we've said before: women are looking to you to see how well the interaction is going. If you seem confident about it, if you seem playful and if you don't seem worried, then most of the time she is going to be okay too.

RON: In the end, it seemed really natural to ask for the phone number. I mean, it was true—we were having a good time and I did want to get to know her better so I asked her if she would like to go out. It wasn't forced. It felt natural.

So often our students worry too much during flirting interactions. They seem to think, "Well, I want to do it perfectly, so every word needs to line up with every other word and it has to be exactly right."

That simply isn't true. As you read these flirting interactions, we hope you're starting to understand that flirting is not a matter of "doing it perfectly." It's a matter of showing up, risking, being curious, committing yourself to being a source of certainty that it's going to be okay and having some fun with it. You'll see again and again that we haven't rewritten these flirting dialogs to make them letter-perfect because that's not how life is, and you shouldn't get the idea that it ever goes perfectly. You'll see that it's not necessary for Romantic Conversations to be perfect for flirting and seduction to work. As you practice you'll have more fun and you will be a lot more seductive.

WHaT KIND OF ADVENTURE WOULD BE FUN?

In this example, Ron is going to talk to Terri again. In this conversation, he's going to ask the Romantic Question "What kind of adventure would be fun?" Notice how this question opens her up. It is not necessarily something that is going to make her melt with romantic feelings, like a question about her most romantic date might, but it is also low-risk and effective. Here it is:

RON: It sounds like you also value fun.

TERRI: Yes.

RON: I've been thinking about the places that I like to go for adventures. You know—the kind of places where you can go and it's really special, fun, exciting and away from your normal daily life. So if I was taking you out what kind of an adventure would be really fun for you? Would it be a day trip together?

TERRI: Yes, a day trip outside or a drive somewhere in the country or a hike in some woods, somewhere there is a nice view, you know? And we could sit on the hillside in the sun and listen to the wind through the tall grass or leaves...

RON: Wow, that sounds great. Have you done any hiking in the mountains or has it been more around here?

TERRI: I've hiked in Hawaii and Alaska but most of my hiking has been in Wisconsin. There are no mountains here.

RON: So traveling is a great passion of yours, is it? Like seeing new places and going to new exciting outdoor places, like in Alaska?

TERRI: Yes, I spent three weeks in Alaska.

RON: Wow, what was that like?

TERRI: It was great, just driving around camping in the different parts of the state. I took a train from Anchorage to Fairbanks and that was a wonderful experience, just seeing the middle of the wilderness from the window of a train.

RON: I don't get to meet a lot of women who are such serious go-getters or have that much guts, so I really admire that about you, that you are able to go on these fun adventures, you know?

TERRI: It is fun, I do like that.

Let's jump in here again and talk about how Ron is doing, flirting with Terri. Ron is really curious, and his curiosity really helps guide him in the conversation and helps the conversation unfold easily. For instance, when Terri talks about her trip to Alaska, Ron gets curious and asks, "What was that like?" That gives her more opportunity to share about something she cares about. Ron then compliments her by telling her that he doesn't get to meet women like her very often and telling her that he admires her adventuresome spirit. That's a great move—we are always looking for something we can admire about the women we are flirting with, and Ron did a great job admiring Terry.

RON: The other thing that I keep asking myself is "What topic has the juice?" It doesn't matter if I am not interested in Alaska or if I am not interested in traveling; it's what lights her up, it's what gets her going on something she is passionate about. Therefore it's important to me. And if it really does light her up, it will ultimately get me interested, even if I'm not interested at the start.

Let's look at the rest of this conversation. Notice how Ron has fun with Terri and jokes around with her.

TERRI: Hawaii was another favorite spot of mine. Hiking along the coast, you come across a sign that says, "Tidal wave level, stay above this sign." And you hope that there's no tidal wave coming.

RON: That sounds pretty adventuresome. Are you telling me that behind that pretty face of yours is this hellcat, daredevil woman?

TERRI: [Laughs] Well, I am not a daredevil. I do worry about life and limb, but I enjoy adventures. But not bungee jumping.

RON: But you are somebody who pushes the envelope. Admit it—you can admit it to me right now. [She laughs] I mean, it is the truth, you are laughing but it is true, you are the one who goes to the tidal wave. You like to come to the edge where it is just almost safe enough and then get pulled back in, right?

TERRI: Right.

RON: Well, thank you for being honest—we finally get an honest answer out of you! [Both laugh]

Ron's interactions with Terri are great examples of being willing to be playful with a woman and to have fun while conducting Romantic Conversations.

WHAT'S A TOTALLY CAREFREE EXPERIENCE?

This time the Romantic Question is "What's a totally carefree experience for you?"

RON: I was at a dinner party a couple days ago and there were a lot of people and we started talking about moments when people felt carefree with someone of the opposite sex, and this woman was talking about what it is like when she is on a date and how she feels free to just be herself, to maybe kiss a guy out of the blue or to say whatever it is she wants to say. I'd be curious to know, if you care to share—what's a totally carefree experience for you?

URSULA: Making love.

RON: Wow, great! That's what I like to hear!

URSULA: Well really, it is just a very free experience with somebody, with someone who enjoys it.

RON: Someone like me?

URSULA: Someone who enjoys it.

RON: I enjoy it, Ron Louis enjoys it.

URSULA: Someone who fully enjoys it with me and who is really with me. Because some people have sex and they are not really with you, but there is this other thing where you're really tuned into each other and you are totally communicating with your entire body, including your eyes, and speaking and everything, and you are using every one of your physical senses with the other person—it is just like nirvana to me, I just think it is nirvana. Have you experienced that?

RON: I have.

URSULA: I have too. I mean, that is the one time I really feel really carefree—when I am with a man I love.

This is a good example of being playful with a woman, being sexy and having fun. You can tell Ron is not going to end up just a friend with this woman.

RON: I was shocked with the answer she gave me to the question—I had no idea that she was going to respond with something so sexual. I remember saying to myself, "I can't believe she is saying this." So I was shocked about that. And that added to the fun of it.

Of course, you're going to get a wide variety of responses from women. Some women will be this responsive, some will be totally unresponsive. This is the great thing about having a high level of "throughput" with women and having a lot of women in your system. When your numbers are good and you know how to talk to women, you'll be able to find and focus on the ones who are the most responsive, which makes everything in the seduction a lot easier. When you find the ones that are that responsive, you go for them and you let go of the ones who are resistant.

WHat are intensely passionate moments for you?

In this example notice how David gets curious about what the woman is saying, how he gets playful and how he asks questions to take the interaction further.

DAVID: I've been sort of conducting an informal survey about this and it's led to some pretty interesting conversations. For whatever reason, there are times when you feel really connected to someone else—it may not be sexual, it could be anywhere, but you just for whatever reason feel really connected and really passionate. So I'd like to ask you: what are some moments in your life where you feel intensely passionate and really connected to somebody else?

CAROL: I just love it when you are having a really deep conversation with somebody and everything else tunes out. I mean, it can happen at a party, for instance. There can be all kinds of people around you, and noise, or it could be just the two of you alone. The important thing is the two of you are having this conversation and suddenly everything else tunes out.

DAVID: Does that happen often for you?

CAROL: Not really.

DAVID: It's happening right now, isn't it?

CAROL: [Laughs] I just love that, when you are really communicating with somebody and you are getting into the conversation and it just goes deeper and deeper and you are really talking heart to heart and you feel completely with the other person, inside the other person, and again, it is just that great thing where all of a sudden everybody else at the party just disappears and just the two of you are suddenly there by yourself even though there is this big bunch of noise going on around you. It's like all of a sudden it's very quiet.

DAVID: Very cool.

CAROL: Yes, and that is just an ideal kind of thing to have in a relationship.

This went really great. This woman is very responsive. Carol described the kind of moment where she was able to feel passionately connected, and it was fun and it created a great, romantic feeling between the two of them. She also gave David some great information: she kept emphasizing the importance of a man being with her. David will be able to use this information in building a connection with her, and use that phrase when he describes that experience to her. He can tell her how important it is for him to feel like he is with her and more importantly can prove that by creating a connection where she really feels like he is with her.

What Are Your Favorite Romantic Movies?

Now Ron is going to ask Sue about romantic movies. Notice how he structures the question with the excuse and the description. At this point they have been having a Romantic Conversation for a while and she is pretty lit up. She is very responsive and obviously likes him. There is definitely a sexual vibe; he has done all of the things to take himself out of the friend category.

RON: I watch a lot of movies. I am kind of a movie buff.

SUE: Me too.

RON: I'm curious about what women feel are romantic movies, romantic characters or situations they feel are romantic, because all women seem to have a different definition of romance.

SUE: Really?

RON: Some women like it when a guy is a great dancer, some like it when a guy is a great father, you never know what a woman will find romantic in a movie. So I would be curious to know, what are some of your favorite romantic movies?

SUE: One that comes to mind is *The English Patient*.

RON: Oh yes.

SUE: That was very romantic.

RON: Was that because of the scene, the romance of the filming or the sensuality of it or was it something else?

Sue says that *The English Patient* is her idea of a really romantic film. Rather than argue with her about it—to us, *The English Patient* was mostly gloomy, actually—Ron got curious. What about this gloomy film did she find romantic? And how will knowing that help him build a connection with her that is both romantic and seductive?

SUE: There were a couple of really romantic relationships in the movie, and one was between the married women and Ralph.

RON: So you can relate to the women who was married, yet she was sleeping with somebody else?

SUE: Yes. Forgetting the marriage part of it, they had an overwhelming physical passion for each other, and that was just very, very exciting in the movie. And then there was this other relationship. They just had to be together, that's all.

RON: And I thought that was very romantic that they go through all this stuff to try to be together. And then there was that romance between the nurse and this Indian soldier.

SUE: Did you think that was romantic? Oh, like there was this one scene, it was so great—he puts candles out all the way from the house she was living in all the way to the barn where he is staying. It was just really great. She comes out and it was a path for her to follow right to him. And I think that was the first night they made love, they had candles all over and it was really romantic.

RON: So you are an old-fashioned romantic, the classic romantic. I am just using these tips for myself so when we get together later I will know to light candles all over the bedroom and to have a trail of candles for you.

SUE: Yeah, and dress yourself up, you know? Wear something really sexy, something special. Put the aftershave on.

RON: Have the wine ready for you.

SUE: Yes, exactly.

RON: It's going to be a good night, it's going to be a good night.

SUE: Chocolates, chocolates.

RON: So you love chocolates?

SUE: Yes, chocolate is supposed to be an aphrodisiac, you know.

RON: Yes, it is supposed to be, we can find out.

SUE: That must be why I like it.

As you can see, things are really cooking between the two of them so Ron is able to push it further by making references to the great time they are going to have together and to actually being in bed together. They are strongly sexual references, but because of the connection they have built through the Flirting Moves and Romantic Questions she was absolutely fine with them.

RON: Yes, I was thinking, "How am I going to make this real? How can I take everything she said about what she finds romantic in these movies, how can I bring those images together with images of her and me together?" So I checked it out—I described us together in a bedroom together with a trail of candles—and she liked it!

Notice how Ron risked rejection, but in a context in which a rejection would most likely not have been personal or harsh. If the woman wasn't interested in him romantically, she could very easily have simply given a tepid answer to Ron's remarks about being in the bedroom with her. She could have said, "Well, that wouldn't work with me" or "I'd have to know someone a long time before that would ever happen" and it wouldn't have even been a blanket rejection of him. It just would have been another piece of information about her, another part of the conversation. Instead, she went right along with it, talking about chocolate and aphrodisiacs. It really pushed everything to the next level. Ron can be fairly assured at this point that she will respond positively when he goes for the first kiss and more.

WHat was your most passionate crush? WHat is your favorite moment in a kiss?

Ron is going to start by asking Terri a Romantic Question about her most passionate crushes. When that does not go exactly where he expects it to go, notice how he moves into the first-kiss questions. The point is, you can tie Romantic Questions together. There is no law saying you can only do one and you have to force an answer. If it looks like something else would work better once you have started on one, go to another. It's not a big deal.

Let's check it out.

RON: I was thinking the other day. I was remembering when I was younger, in high school, and I was thinking about some of the women I had crushes on and how nerve-wracking it was, feeling exciting and vulnerable. What are some moments that you can remember in your life, like when you had a crush on somebody back then and what happened?

TERRI: Oh, wow.

RON: Like the first guy you had a crush on, what was it like?

TERRI: In kindergarten?

RON: I was thinking about in high school, but kindergarten is fine. Kindergarten, you started early!

TERRI: I had two boyfriends in kindergarten, but they had the same name so it wasn't real confusing. High school, I had crushes on boys, but usually nothing came of it.

RON: Come on, let's get some names.

TERRI: So there would be Tom. Yes, I had a crush on him.

RON: What became of it?

TERRI: Something did happen there. We went steady for six months when I was 13 years old.

RON: What was a crush where you looked at the guy like you are looking at me and you just felt like your heart pitter patter, and that kind of thing.

TERRI: Oh, let's see, there was a Tom, that's for sure. There were a lot of Bobs, too.

RON: I was thinking about this too: the moments you are kissing and you are passionately lost and you are saying to yourself "This is great" and it is so fulfilling to be with them and you are with them and your eyes are closed and you are just lost, just getting into the experience of it. What are times for you, if you are willing to share how you feel, was it recently when you have had that feeling of enjoying like your favorite part of the kiss?

TERRI: What is my favorite part of a kiss? Well, my favorite part of a kiss is someone that knows how to kiss, that helps. And—

RON: You are blushing a little bit!

TERRI: I am. [Smiles]

RON: The chemistry is there.

TERRI: So yes, someone who knows how to kiss. I love to kiss.

RON: Tell me some of the moments, if you are willing to. Let's say we are kissing and your eyes are closed. Would this be a moment in the kiss that was great? Would it be at the beginning, the middle or...?

TERRI: It would be after a little amount of time, but not a lot. You find out really quickly if the kiss is great.

RON: All right, great, I understand that. You can show me this later.

Ron started with a Romantic Question about crushes but it didn't really get to the kind of intensity that he was looking for. He was looking for a response like "Wow, with my first crush in high school, Bob, I couldn't stop thinking about him and we couldn't keep our hands off each other." Instead, he kept getting somewhat vague and innocent childhood crushes.

This is fine, and it's exactly the sort of thing that will happen with women on a regular basis. The woman you are flirting with probably has not read this book, so she may not know the responses she's "supposed" to give. Put another way, these techniques work in broad strokes—the woman you are with may well be unresponsive to certain questions or may wander off topic or whatever. In this case, Ron decided to shift to another question, about the best moment of a kiss, because there wasn't much juice with the first-crush question. And it worked—almost immediately things started going deeper and he was able to make a flirting remark about how she could show him the best moment of a kiss later on. Had she been a little more responsive he could have even gone for giving her the first kiss at that point.

What's Your Favorite Vacation Spot?

David's Romantic Question, about Heather's favorite vacation spot, leads into a lot of different topics and into a lot of different opportunities to flirt. Also notice how easily the question draws her into talking about things she cares about and about memories that are pleasant to her. All these good feelings are getting connected to David, leaving her liking him more and wanting to be with him.

DAVID: So I was watching this travel show the other night and I was wondering about vacations and about how I haven't been on a vacation in a while. I was wondering if you have a favorite vacation spot or vacation dream? You know, perhaps a place you have been that blew you away or a place where you really sort of just let go. Or maybe a place where you would really like to go. I was just kind of curious about your thoughts about your ideal vacation.

HEATHER: I really like to travel. I went to Ireland about a year ago, and that was pretty much the ideal vacation. I went with a couple of friends and it was a really great trip. We didn't plan things out—instead of having this huge itinerary we just did what we wanted when we wanted to. That's what I like to do when I am traveling. I don't like to have to be somewhere at a certain time, that's how things are in my life at home. So it is really nice to be able to just stay somewhere if you like it or leave if you don't.

DAVID: I bet you get to have experiences that way that you would not otherwise have. You get to see things that normal tourists would not get to see.

HEATHER: Yes. I think my ideal vacation is about having some time to rest and meeting new people and getting a feel for the culture wherever I am. It's about seeing the countryside, hiking, walking.

Let's jump in a second. David is doing some cool stuff with this woman and it's working. First, he found out where her ideal vacation was. Once he had that he started asking her about the best moment on that vacation, the one moment when she felt most special and amazed and when she felt like her life was absolutely at its best. He let himself get curious and ask follow-up questions. You can see how that is helping the whole conversation unfold in an interesting manner.

We should mention here that "favorite vacation" is not a very risky Romantic Question in that it does not automatically let her know you are romantically interested in her in the way that a question like "What is your idea of a perfect romantic date?" would. That's okay, because this Romantic Question does not exist in a void. Along with the Romantic Question, David is doing the Flirting Moves. Also, he will ask her other Romantic Questions that build in intensity and riskiness as his interactions with her unfold.

David is also getting lots of information about her. He's learning how she likes to relax: she doesn't like regimented relaxation; she likes to be able to hang out and be spontaneous. This information will be helpful to him when he starts designing their Seduction Date: he'll be sure to set up a date where she has options and where they can "follow their noses" rather than one that is more tightly regimented or structured. (You can read more about seduction dates in our book *How to Succeed with Women,* and in our other products.)

Let's get back to their conversation.

DAVID: Was there one place that you went to where you thought something like "Wow, this is so special, this is so amazing"? Or was there one experience you had, maybe sitting on the beach, where you felt like "Wow, I am here! This is my life, this is amazing." Maybe it was someone you met, I don't know.

HEATHER: I think it was when we were hiking around in a national forest. It was really beautiful. It was hard to believe I was really there. I kept telling myself that I was in Ireland. It was really magical and beautiful. There were waterfalls and rolling hills and a lake and it was really beautiful.

And another time was when we were near a little town and we were driving along the coastline on this narrow little dirt road, it is just a really bizarre driving experience. We reached a place where the whole road was taken up by a large herd of cattle.

DAVID: Wow.

HEATHER: I guess they regularly do that, move them from one part of the field to another.

DAVID: So they were just hanging out in the road?

HEATHER: I guess that was the only way. There was this little boy with a stick trying to get them in line and trying to get them to turn the corner to go on this other road and it was just very memorable. That would never happen around here, and it was just a really funny experience.

DAVID: Yes, wow. That sounds great, like one of those simple, perfect moments you'll remember forever and always feel good about. I often think about those moments when you feel like you really have lived life. You know, those moments that later in your life you look back on and you are really happy that you took the opportunity that came your way. It sounds like you are pretty happy you took that opportunity to go on that trip and to find out what there was in it for you. So what about your future? Are there places that you fantasize about going to that really turn you on to think about?

Let's break in again. David found out about her past favorite vacation, which led to her sharing a simple, wonderful moment that she will always remember. Now David's curiosity has taken him in the direction of the future.

HEATHER: I have always wanted to go to Nova Scotia. I really don't know a lot about it but I'm interested in the music I've heard from that region, and I understand that a lot of people who live there have Scottish ancestors.

DAVID: Oh, wow.

HEATHER: And I have heard that the countryside is really beautiful and that the music is great. Like I said before, one of the best things about traveling is meeting people who are there.

DAVID: I can tell you are someone who really cares about connecting with people, making real connections. I find that really attractive, so that is really a cool thing.

David ended by admiring something about her—that she really cares about making real connections, which happens to be true, and by telling her that he found that attractive, which also happens to be true. In this way he made the Romantic Question even more romantic by finding her interest, admiring it and telling her that because of it she's the kind of woman to whom he's attracted. These last moves took the whole inter-action to a more personal level.

What Was It Like When You Knew You Were In Love?

Now we're going to hear Ron talk to Terri and ask her some more Romantic Questions. You'll notice that at the beginning he gives the excuse and the question, but not the description. The reason for that is that he is in the flow with her and the conversation, so there is some flexibility. Until you get good at it, you really should do all three parts of the Romantic Question.

Also, notice that Ron uses the question "Do you believe in love at first sight?" Watch carefully how he does that, because, as you probably know, if you go up to a woman in a bar and say, "Hey baby, do you believe in love at first sight?" you will probably get nothing more from her than a drink thrown in your face. But if you structure it properly, the way he does it here, you can really get a conversation going. He doesn't lead with that question but builds up to it, so it seems quite natural.

RON: You know, I was talking to a friend of mine and we were talking about different times she has been in love and what it was like, and so I would be curious to know what are times in your life when you suddenly felt like you knew you were in love?

TERRI: Oh wow, how many do you want to know about?

RON: I just want to know about one or two. I can recall what it was like when you say to yourself, "This person is great" and you love being with them and it is almost like the world becomes a rosy picture.

TERRI: Right, "This person is perfect." The chemistry is there, the common interests are there, the wit and warmth and playfulness are there. The playfulness is important, so those things come together, and so you say, "This is it, this is great."

RON: So it is great.

TERRI: You just go around and gush.

RON: Do you believe in love at first sight? Is that possible?

TERRI: Oh yes.

RON: Is it happening right now, as we speak?

TERRI: [Laughs] I'm not going to tell you that!

RON: What are the secrets? Does it happen to you, love at first sight or lust at first sight?

TERRI: Lust at first sight, yes, love at first sight, no. It might take a couple of sights, though.

RON: A couple of moments?

TERRI: Yes, pretty quickly, usually in a few days.

WHat Are your Favorite Romantic Dates?

This time, Ron is talking to Terri and he is going to ask her about romantic evenings together. One thing to notice is how he brings the things she says back to his relationship with her and its inevitable success by saying things like "You are giving me lots of good tips on where I can take you."

RON: I would be curious, what are some of the best first dates you've ever been on? When you meet someone and it is going great and you might meet for coffee—like we might be doing soon—and things are good and then you go out on a more romantic date. What are some romantic dates you can recall that went great?

TERRI: Starting out with dinner and just walking around, maybe downtown, and seeing the night sky from various places, sort of checking out what's here, what's there, what new clubs are there. Just kind of exploring together. Then walking back to the car and thinking, "I don't want to go home" and he says to me, "Do you want to go home yet?" and I say, "No, not me." Just continuing, finding a quiet place... Going to each club, opening the door, saying, "No, too loud," closing the door and moving on to the next one. Just not wanting the evening to end, just being together, just talking and walking.

RON: So what is it about that that is so amazing to you? You were together walking around, and what is it about that that is so romantic or sensual to you?

TERRI: Just the wanting to stay together, wanting to know more about the other person to sort of gradually getting closer, just sort of bumping into each other just sort of holding hands, just step by step, physically getting a lit bit closer, learning more and more and being outdoors too, just enjoying the night sky and enjoying the sights and sounds together. If you were in some exotic place, you would probably lose your focus, I think, on the other person.

RON: So you are giving me a lot of good tips on where I can take you, is that what you are telling me?

TERRI: Right.

This woman gave Ron a lot of information when he asked about her ideal romantic date, and he got curious and wanted to boil it down to the bottom line. So he asked her, "So what is it about that that is so amazing to you?" And that deepened her even more into the feeling she liked so much.

It's worth noting that you can use the question "What is it about that?" any time a woman is describing an experience that she enjoyed. She enjoys going from club to club, just walking around with a guy? Asking "What is it about that that was so great?" will help her focus even more on those feelings you want her to be having with you.

If you listen to a woman's answers to your Romantic Questions, she will often outline what her ideal date is. You will then use that information when you construct a seduction date with her. In this case, Terry is telling Ron that one thing that might make her happy is walking around downtown, holding hands and exploring. He's created a connection with her, created some romantic feelings and discovered a potential plan for seducing her. Great!

WHat is your Favorite moment in a Kiss?

DAVID: I was talking to a friend of mine recently about kissing. We were watching an old movie on TV where there was a lot of kissing going on and we got into a conversation about the whole lost art of kissing. You know, people don't think about that enough.

SUE: Oh, I agree.

DAVID: I like everything that your normal guy likes, but sometimes I think I like kissing more than your average guy does.

SUE: Oh, that's great.

DAVID: I was thinking about this: what is your favorite moment in a kiss? There are so many different stages to a kiss, you know? Like you are about to kiss, then you start to kiss, then you are really into the kiss, then there's the first moment your tongues touch... And you could be kissing someone and the world just seems to stop, you know? So what is your favorite moment in a kiss?

SUE: I just love that very first instant when your lips come together. There is nothing like it. It gets good after that too. But you know, you are separate, you are separate, you are separate, then you get closer, closer, closer, you know you are going to kiss and then you know the lips touch. Oh, to me that's just sensational.

DAVID: Have you ever had one of those times where you are about to kiss somebody and it's winter and there's static electicity and there is a little spark from your lips to theirs, right before your kiss?

SUE: [Laughs] I think that has happened. But I think it was his braces.

DAVID: That moment just before it happens is my favorite moment too, I think.

SUE: Yes, just the very instant when your lips first touch.

DAVID: Especially for the first time with someone and you really like them and you really trust them.

SUE: Especially if they know how to kiss. I mean, I have been out with men that have been married and do not know how to kiss.

Things are going great. She's responsive to the question, so that's really great news, and she's getting used to sharing on this level about such intimate topics and having it be a good time.

We'll talk more later about the first kiss, but for now, notice how this Romantic Question could lead to a first-kiss situation. As they share more deeply about kissing, and as the vibe becomes more intimate, it would be a simple matter for David to lean over and say something like "What a great idea, I think I'll kiss you right now" and do it.

DAVID: So how do you kiss? What would your advice be for me? Let's say you and I are kissing, hypothetically, and if we got to know each other that way, what would be a good kiss?

SUE: Well, I don't like a first kiss where your mouth is hanging completely open. That is just too much too soon. That is just gross. Your lips should be just slightly parted, and your lips need to be very relaxed and flexible. When you touch each other's lips, you should try to make the whole lip touch their whole lip. And then you can just slightly move your lips, like a gentle massaging kind of movement, so you are really using your lips like fingers. You know, you are really filling up the person's lips with your lips, if you can imagine.

DAVID: I can imagine, you are making me want to try that out, practice my kissing.

This is a spot where actually taking that first kiss would be a fine thing to do. David could lean across and say, "You mean, something like this?" and kiss her exactly as she described.

WHat are your Favorite Romantic movies?

DAVID: I have been watching a lot of different movies lately. I've been in sort of a film-festival mode around my house. I mean, I like action films but also have been getting into more romantic kind of films, like *When Harry Met Sally*.

SUE: I like that one.

DAVID: I just love those scenes where a woman is being swept off her feet and just really able to just totally let go into some sort of whirlwind romance. And I was just wondering, what are some of your favorite romantic scenes or romantic movies?

SUE: Well, you know, I am glad you mentioned *When Harry Met Sally*, cause it is one of my favorite movies. And I have a favorite scene too—it is when Harry and Sally are at a New Year's Eve party but they are not in a relatonship with each other, but they have both tried relationships with other people, and there is a moment when Harry, all of a sudden he looks at her and he realizes that she is the one and that he loves her. He gets a look on his face, you can read his mind, he is just like looking at her with love in his eyes.

DAVID: Wow, that's really cool. I have also been looking at some of the Cary Grant movies. Like him and Audrey Hepburn in *Charade*.

SUE: Oh, *Charade!* That is one of my favorite movies, I have that movie.

DAVID: I would love to see that film again: the way they play together and how Cary Grant is always changing identies and they have such fast rapport and are so witty.

SUE: That is such a great movie, and romantic. It is so clever and romantic. I really love all the movies Cary Grant made, I really love *To Catch A Thief*. There is a great moment when Grace Kelly just kisses the heck out of him.

DAVID: Yep, I remember that.

SUE: She just like takes him. That is a great scene.

DAVID: What is that great movie he made with Ingrid Bergman?

SUE: He was pretending to be a married man so he would not get committed in his relationships. I can't think of the name but that is a really good movie.

DAVID: Well, it's good to get connected to a women who knows some of those films. You know what I think would be fun one night is to get together, cuddle up together, get some popcorn and watch *Charade* or something like that.

SUE: Yes, that would be fun.

Conclusion

You now know about asking Romantic Questions. You have seen the spectrum of risk that those questions can cover and how they create conversation, intimacy and openings for going deeper into your connections with a woman. You've seen how using Romantic Questions does a lot to keep you out of the friends zone and creates conversations that a friend would never have with a woman.

The next step: taking talking further. •

How to Talk to Women

CHapter 12
TAKING TALKING FUrTHer

There are other important steps to seducing a woman beyond simply being able to talk to her. You need to get her number or email address and set up the date. You need to be able to talk to her on the date— okay, we've covered that in exhaustive detail!—and you need to be able to go for the first kiss.

In our dating coaching practice, we get lots of questions about these issues, so the first part of this chapter will be in question and answer format. Then we'll talk about going for the first kiss.

For further information about everything covered in this chapter and to learn about where to meet women, Priming Dates, Seduction Dates and much, much more, check out our book *How to Succeed with Women*, and, of course, our website, howtosucceedwithwomen.com.

HOW to ask for the PHONE number

Men often ask us how to get a woman's number or ask her out. There's no trick to it, as you'll see from this Q & A.

QUESTION: Hey guys—I just wanted to ask how to close the deal with a girl. After talking to them for a while I still have trouble getting their numbers or asking them out on dates. I would appreciate your advice.

ANSWER: This is simpler than you might think. After chatting with a woman for a while and doing some of the flirting moves so she knows you're interested, you simply say, "Hey, you seem cool. What would it be like if we went out for a cup of coffee sometime? Could I have your email address or phone number?" If she says yes, try to set up the date right then.

It's really just a matter of opening your mouth (or, as Ron calls it, your "pie trap") and risking rejection by asking her.

USING THE PHONE TO ASK OUT WOMEN

Many a successful date lives or dies on how you use the phone. You'll see in these questions that we consistently give one piece of advice: get her email address!

Q: I really like this girl in school (we are both in college). I think she is responsive whenever I talk with her and I don't think she has a boyfriend. I got her number and she said I could call her, but I've called several times and she hasn't called back. What should I do? Should I leave her alone?

A: When a woman doesn't call you back, it does not mean that she isn't interested in you. Never expect a woman to call you back, especially at the beginning of your seduction of her. Shocking as it may seem, a woman who is interested in you will very likely not call back. Of course, neither will a woman who is not interested, so you just can't use callback frequency as a measure of how much she likes you.

So when should you call her? When you want to. But don't keep leaving messages—simply call. If she answers, great, but only leave a message once in a while. If after the third message she hasn't called you back, she's not interested, and that's too bad. Time to move on.

Sadly, the phone can become a real stumbling block. Don't worry that she might think you are weird for calling—remember, she's looking to you to see whether or not she should feel weird about things. If you don't think it's weird to call her, odds are she won't, either.

This problem points to the importance of getting her email address. Set up the date via email or a combination of email and telephone and you'll be way ahead of the game.

Q: How do I deal with answering machines when trying to set up a time and date for the Priming Date? I hate to keep calling, trying to catch her in person, especially because Caller ID and *69 can make it sooo easy to find out who just called you.

A: This is a real problem and can kill a romance before it even gets started. However, there is a way to block caller ID. It varies from area to area, but it's often accomplished by dialing *67, then the number—caller ID shows you as "Private Number." Dial *67, then the number. If you get the machine, hang up. Check your phone book before trying this; *67 may not work in all areas.

Of course, this doesn't mean you shouldn't ever leave a message. Just don't leave more than three of them. And how you do this depends a lot on how hot a lead the woman is. If you have great rapport with her and have flirted with her many times and it's pretty clear she's just being scatterbrained, you can say something like "I have to tell you, I have a policy. I don't mean to be mean, but I can't leave more than three messages without getting a call back. If you don't get back to me, I won't be able to call you for a long time. I like you and you seem like a great woman, but that's just what's up. Anyway, my number is…" This isn't heavy; you're not yelling at her…just telling her the way it is. You aren't upset, just stating the facts.

If she doesn't return your calls after three messages, we think she's probably not interested. If you see her, don't mention the calls—do not confront her about it! Flirt with her more and try to set up a date right then!

Q: Since I began studying *How to Succeed with Women* about a year and a half ago, over and over again, I've become extremely successful. I've reached the point where I can get almost any single woman's phone number and I now have a high success rate of having sex on dates.

However, the big snag I'm hitting lately is after getting the girl's number. I've had about 10 girls over the past month who seem very attracted to me give up the phone number, then either never call back or make up stupid excuses to not go out. I'm used to having at least three dates per week and I've had none for several weeks now, so it's frustrating.

A: You certainly are having some solid success, and that is great. What you are bumping up against is a very common pattern we've noticed with our students: success and failure seem to come in waves. That's part of the seduction life. By waves, we mean that there seem to be trends in dating that are outside of your control, based in some sort of randomness or luck. And it's weird: some-times every woman calls back—sometimes none do. Sometimes every woman you date wants to sleep with you. Sometimes there are periods of no sex. Sometimes every woman you interact with is a blonde. Sometimes they all seem to be schoolteachers. Strange though these trends may seem, they are normal. And in time, the trends always turn.

In the meantime, here are some other pointers we invite you to reflect on:

- How long do you wait to call the woman after you get the num-ber? Perhaps you are waiting too long to call and set up the date. Maybe you should try to tie down the date at the same time you get the phone number.

- Are you actively doing the three-step rejection process when things don't work out or are you getting demoralized?

In case you've forgotten, the three-step rejection process is:

1. Remember that dating is a numbers game. You will probably have to hear a certain number of nos before you get a yes, so this is one more no you won't have to hear again on your way to the inevitable yes from someone else.

2. Change your interpretation of why she rejected you from something that has to do with you to something that has to do with her or with life. "I guess she didn't hear me." "Looks like she's wrapped up in her own world." "Perhaps her dog just died." Remember, just because an explanation is painful doesn't mean you have to believe it. Find an explanation that is not painful for you and practice believing that.

3. Redirect your attention to something else. Don't dwell in the rejection—find something else—anything else—and let yourself get absorbed in it.

- If they don't call you back, do you then assume they are not interested and not call them again? We recommend that you expect them not to call you back and that you call a number of times— say, three times—before you give up on them. With each call, act as though the previous call never happened. Never confront a woman about not calling you back.

- Do you ever get their email addresses? This might be a more effective way to seduce them. If they are busy maybe email is more efficient—and you can use Romantic Questions, Deepening and other seduction moves to "pre-seduce" them via email before the date.

Taking Things Further Via Email

Q: When is a good time to start sending romantic letters via email? I have known this girl for about two weeks. Extremely hot. I have to shake guys' hands everywhere I go just because they have seen me with her. I don't want to push it too fast with the romantic talk, but I also want her to think romantically about me. I also have her home address if you would like to add anything there...

A: Good work on the first steps—going out with a woman you find attractive. Now for the next step—turning mindless hanging out into something romantic and sexual.

You don't say much about your relationship now. What's it like? Are you kissing? Making out? Having sex? Heck, are you even holding hands? Does she know you are not just a friend? This stuff is important.

Since you are reluctant to make romantic talk with her, we can deduce that you are probably not having sex with her. You must start showing your romantic interest in her. You must be compliment-ing her, for one thing. If you are not complimenting her as a woman or showing your romantic interest then you are really in trouble—she may be thinking of you as a friend already.

Email is great because it gives you the opportunity to say things, especially romantic things, that you might not normally have the nerve to say to a woman. It gives you an opportunity to run "visual-izations" on her. Remember, when you describe something to someone, she has to go inside and imagine what you are describing just to be able to track with what you are talking about. If I describe a cow, you have to imagine it. By the same token, if you describe an experience to someone, she has to go inside and imagine having that experience in order to understand what you are talking about. So you want to write emails that describe wonderful feelings of love and romance to the woman of your dreams. This will get her in the right state of mind for your next move.

We suggest love poems. Search online or go to a bookstore or library and look under love poetry. Write her emails that say things like "I saw this poem and it made me think of you. I thought I'd share it." Then enclose the poem. Feel free to use the same poem on a number of women, just so long as they don't know each other.

In your situation, romantic emails should be part of your approach. You should be showing your romantic interest and taking her on a Seduction Date. You should have an outcome in mind for each date—kissing her? having sex? Be sure to pursue other women—don't let her be your one-and-only hope—and be willing to risk finding out what she thinks of you. If you haven't kissed her yet, you should soon. Whatever you do, don't let this thing remain "maybe friends, maybe potential lovers." Be the man, push the situation and find out.

Taking Things Farther

Q: How can I go from hand-holding to something more intense? I find I can get to the point where I'm sitting on the couch with a woman, watching a movie and holding hands. But what next?

A: You've heard the saying "God is in the details"? Well, so is sex, as it turns out. If you can bring exquisite, detailed attention to even a tiny part of her body, she'll go nuts for more. The mistake most men make is they want to move on to something big—and fast. To advance from hand-holding to something more, you have to focus on being small and slow.

This means slowly caressing the palm of her hand or touching your fingertips to hers and really bringing your attention to the feeling of the sensation. Or you might just lightly stroke the inside of her wrist. You do this to draw her attention to the subtleties of the touch you are sharing. Also, take your time with it. Most of our students are afraid that if they don't rush sexual interactions, sex will never happen. But it turns out the opposite is true. If you show that you are really willing to give her detailed, attentive touching and that you aren't pushing things, it will very often draw her towards you. Also, if you are willing to show that you have some faith that sex will happen—you show this by not pushing things too hard, or too fast— you will be very attractive to her. You won't be like all the bone-headed guys who either are friends because they show no interest at all or are jerks because they try to push her into sex.

You may also want to hold eye contact while you are doing this touching. Don't force it: if she turns to look at you, hold her gaze. Be willing to look into her eyes and to have her look into yours. Show her you are willing to hold that intimate contact. She'll probably be looking to you for whether it's okay or not to connect so strongly, so let yourself believe that it's okay—don't wait for her to believe it's fine before you do.

This is a good time to comment on the energy between you. Commenting on the energy draws her attention to it without it seeming like you are forcing anything. Saying, "Wow, this energy between us is really amazing" can do a lot to intensify her awareness and acceptance of that energy. If she says, "Yes, it really feels great," that's when you might want to kiss her. You can either slowly lean in and kiss her without saying anything or use the announcement method and say something like "Don't panic, I'm going to kiss you now."

Commenting on the energy is also a great test to see whether she is ready for the first kiss or not. If she says, "Eh, I don't feel much energy," then you know to not bother trying to kiss her. If she says, "Yes, I feel it and it really scares me, I think we should slow things down," then you know to back off for a while until she is comfortable. Often women will pose some sort of problem at this point to see how you will handle it: "Will he be patient with me or will he argue, pout or be a jerk?" Be patient, don't resist her resistance and go back to hand-holding. Move closer again later.

These steps will help build the real energy and intimacy between you and open the gateway for more contact.

Turning A Friend Into A Lover

Sometimes men want to take talking further when they haven't even done the appropriate talking first. If a woman thinks of you as a friend and you are interested in her romantically then you must take action to take things farther. Here's a question about that.

Q: Is it possible to turn a woman from a friend into a lover even if you've known her as a friend for a few months?

A: Yes, it is possible to turn a woman from a friend to a lover if you know what to do—but even then it won't work every time. Some women keep you as a friend because you've been too scared to make your romantic interest known or because you've made a bunch of bonehead mistakes and alienated her (at least temporarily) from being romantic. Perhaps you've made fart jokes, said callous things or treated her like a buddy—nothing too serious. These are women you've got a shot at changing into lovers.

Other women have you squarely in the just friends category, and you ain't goin' anywhere, pal. These women may be married or in relationships, they may be difficult, high-maintenance women or— the sad fact—they simply may not like you very much and just keep you around for when they have nothing better to do. You are unlikely to turn these women into lovers, but by trying, at least you'll get them out of your life and clear some psychic space for women who do want to be sexual with you.

So what can you do to get "just a friend" to become your lover? Let's look at the basic primer on friends-to-lovers, Louis & Copeland style.

Pursue other women. If you want to turn a friend into a lover, it is crucial beyond words that she not be your one-and-only-hope for sex. You must be pursuing other women, flirting with other women, romancing other women and being sexual with other women. Pursuing and being successful with other women is the only way to have real freedom around the friend you are trying to seduce. It will give you a sense of patience with her, remove any sense of desperation you may be feeling around her and make you less available—and thus more attractive—to her.

Act like a lover, not like a female friend. Pop quiz, hotshot: what does a man who becomes a woman's friend do differently with her than another woman would? Answer: nothing. Moral: if you want a woman to see you as a sexual man, rather than basically as an ugly woman, then you must act differently than another woman would. This is true for women you are just meeting as well as for women who have known you for a while and already think of you as a friend. Bottom line: you must flirt with her, weird as it may feel to you the first time you do it. You must flirt.

So often a man who ends up a woman's friend falls into the trap of wanting the woman to feel comfortable above all else.

Consequently, he is indecisive and appears weak to her, always nervous, always waiting for her to relax before he relaxes. He doesn't ever flirt or say anything romantic because he doesn't want to risk making her uncomfortable. Only if he has a clear signal that flirting is okay will he do it. This will never work.

If you are going to be seductive with a woman, you must be willing to provide the certainty that everything in the interaction is okay— even if it's romantic. That means that you believe it's okay and let her know it. You don't act like there's a problem—you act like everything is great! Since she's probably been looking to you and your behavior to know how to feel about things, most of the time this will actually help her relax.

You must start doing all the flirting moves. You also must start using the flirting skills. You must ask "What's the story behind that?" You must practice Situational Flirting and the Goodbye Introduction. You must conduct Romantic Conversations and Deepening Conversations. When you start incorporating these behaviors into your life, women will not wonder whether you are a wimpy friend or a potential lover. You'll be a potential lover every time—or she'll get rid of you. (More on that below.)

Be upbeat and be busy. The chances are you are kind of depressed when you're with the female friend you want to have sex with, complaining about your life and generally being a whiner. You must stop doing that right away. She should find herself thinking, "Wow, he seems pretty happy, even without me. I'd better get a piece of that!" rather than "Wow, this guy is a downer." You must act more upbeat, like you have something going on in your life. The best way to do this is to pursue other women (see above).

One man we know did this with a woman he was interested in. She had dated him a few times, then decided they should be just friends. ("I'm very excited," she told him. "I'm excited you are going to be my new best friend." Arrrg!) He started following the dating fundamentals aggressively and soon found himself being sexual with another woman. In that place of sexual abundance, he was able to be happier and less available around the woman who wanted to be just friends.

He told us, "She called to tell me she'd be too busy to see me for a while and I was able to honestly say it was just fine—that I was really looking forward to seeing her and that we'd get together whenever we both found the time. Her response? 'But I really want to see you!' By being happy and busy, I've been able to keep her pursuing me, and I'm confident I'll end up in bed with her." He's free to be patient with her, to work the seduction slowly, and not be attached to the outcome. Be upbeat and busy if you want to turn a friend into a lover.

Refuse to stay just friends. If you do what we say, things will start seeming more romantic with the women you befriended. She'll either get with the program (and probably say, "You've changed!") or she'll tell you in no uncertain terms that you are now and will forever be just friends. If that happens, you have to stop hanging around with her. Without hedging, tell her, "I'm sorry, but it's too painful for me to be just friends with someone I feel this way about. I'm attracted to you." Then stop hanging around with her—at least you'll be doing something positive for your self-esteem as a man.

Don't backslide. If she goes for it and gets romantic with you, you may be tempted to fall into the trap of acting like a friend again. Don't do it! Follow seduction protocol.

THE FIRST KISS

The first kiss can come at any time in an interaction with a woman. This is a critically important point. So many men mess up their seductions of women by thinking the first kiss has to come at the end of the date. They therefore don't have their eyes open for opportunities to go for the kiss earlier and put so much pressure on themselves at the end of the date that they mess up the kiss anyway.

As you practice flirting, you'll find that there are more opportunities to build up to and go for the first kiss than you used to think. For example, we always suggest that you behave like a gentleman with women. If a woman interests you, try to always open doors for her. In a nice restaurant, pull out the chair for her. If she is a passenger in your car, open the door for her and close it for her after she gets in. These little gentleman-ly moves are like the Flirting Moves; they keep reminding her that you are not just a friend. You are a man, treating her like a woman. This will go a long way toward continuing the seduction. In a way, being a gentleman is a form of Situational Flirting, because you are using the elements of the situation you are in as a way of continually showing her your romantic intentions. This can lead to a first kiss.

Here's an example: David was once on a date that had been set up by some friends of his. His two friends (a couple) had decided to play matchmaker and had set up a dinner for the four of them. Now, we always advise our students not to count on their friends to set them up, but at the same time being set up is an acceptable part of your dating strategy. It just should never be your one-and-only hope. We also usually tell men to have Priming Dates before having dinner dates. (A Priming Date is a coffee date you have with a woman. You don't move on to Seduction Dates—basically evening dates—until you've established some mutual sexual interest. See our book *How to Succeed with Women* for much more on Priming Dates and Seduction Dates.)

But few rules are carved in stone, so David went along on this dinner-and-dancing date. It turned out the woman, Betsy, was very pretty and intelligent. They had a good time at dinner; David was flirting with her, smiling, holding eye contact, winking and checking out her body. He asked her "What's the story behind that?" and did some Deepening. He asked the Romantic Question "What is your idea of a most romantic date?" and all four of them discussed it. David noticed that after this, Betsy's eyes sparkled as she looked at him.

After dinner the four of them went dancing. David's friends let David and Betsy off in front of the dance club while they went to park the car. It was cold, so David took off his jacket and put it around Betsy's shoulders as they walked to the club. This was Situational Flirting in that it was using the elements of the situation to show romantic interest (though it wasn't comic, as most Situational Flirting is). As they waited outside the club for their friends, Betsy asked David, "Aren't you cold?" He answered, "Yes, but a kiss would warm me up!" She said, "Okay," and they leaned together and kissed.

At that point, they had known each other about two hours. He had flirted and shown romantic interest and she had responded. Once this kiss had happened, David's question was no longer "Will she get sexual with me?" The question became one of "When?" By paying attention to the environment and using the situation to his advantage, David was able to get the first kiss well before the end of the date—and much more later in the evening.

Here's another example. Ron was on a Priming Date with a woman in a coffee shop. He had done the Flirting Moves and asked his date the Romantic Question "What is your ideal romantic date?" She responded enthusiastically, telling him, "There are actually three ideal scenarios" and describing them in detail. She then asked him about his ideal romantic date, and they looked into each other's eyes as he talked about it.

She excused herself to go to the bathroom. When she came out of the bathroom, she paused in front of the fire burning in the coffee shop's fireplace. Ron came up behind her and gently put his hands on her shoulders. She turned and smiled, looking into his eyes, and they kissed several times. This was after knowing her for about an hour.

One of our students met a woman at a campus grocery co-op. They hit it off and he asked her if she'd like to go to a coffee shop with him. She said yes, so they went to one and talked for over an hour. He did the Flirting Moves and Deepening and asked some Romantic Questions. During a Deepening Conversation he asked her, "What would you most like to be doing with your life?" She answered, and there was a very close, intimate feeling in the air. She asked him the question back. He answered, "I don't know what I want to be doing with my life, but I know that right now I want to be kissing you." She blushed and said, "Okay," and he leaned across and kissed her. From that point on, there was no question that their relationship was romantic, not just friends. Total time from meeting her to getting that first kiss? One hour and 20 minutes.

Does this happen every time? Of course not. But it can happen a lot more than most men realize—but you have to take the opportunity to go for the kiss when it presents itself. Simply having an eye open for opportunity will dramatically increase your chances of getting the first kiss well before the end of the date.

GOING FOR THE FIRST KISS

There are two basic conditions that must be created for the first kiss to work (for a lot more on this, see *How to Succeed with Women*). First, she must not be surprised by the kiss. She must be thinking of it or seeing it as somewhat inevitable. This will happen if you've shown your romantic interest, if you've done what we've outlined in this book, and—here's the X-factor—if she likes you. If you do these things, she's likely to like you, but of course, you never know. The bottom line: if you've shown romantic interest, she shouldn't be surprised when you go to kiss her.

Second, she must like the idea of being kissed. You test this through the flirting and Romantic Conversations that you do. If she resists your flirting—if she won't hold eye contact, glares at you when you check out her body or turns away when you wink—she probably is not interested in the first kiss. If she answers all your Romantic Questions with one-word or evasive replies, she's probably not interested. Don't bother going for the kiss; she's not interested.

If she's been receptive to all the other romantic things you've done then you can go for the first kiss with a good chance of success. There are a couple of ways to do it. You can ask her if you can kiss her, but many women find this offensive, believe it or not. You can "just do it," but when you do, you run the risk of doing it against her will—which is third-degree sexual assault if it pisses her off enough. (Don't say we didn't warn you!) We like simply announcing the kiss by leaning toward her and saying something like "Wow, I'm going to kiss you" or "Don't panic, I'm going to kiss you." This works well and doesn't leave her thinking that you are a beggar or a jerk.

CONCLUSION

Talking to women is not the only component of succeeding with women, though it is a critical part. You still must be able to get her number or email address, set up the date and go for that all-important first kiss. If you add the skills in this chapter to what you now know about talking to women, you'll go a long way toward having the sex life you desire. •

How to Talk to Women

CHapter 13
conclusion

Congratulations! From this moment forward, you never have to feel like you are "stuck" in your talking to women again. You now know the Flirting Moves, "What's the story behind that?," Situational Flirting, Deepening, the Goodbye Introduction, Romantic Questions and more. With these skills available to you, you always have someplace to go in a conversation. You can use your curiosity and ask a question. You can do some Deepening. You can ask a Romantic Question. You can take a risk. You can make sure you are smiling, winking or conveying vitality with your body. As you practice with this material, you will find that there's always a direction you can go in a conversation with a woman, and that is very relaxing knowledge, indeed.

You've also learned that talking to (and seducing) women is a sequence, and the parts of the sequence all fit together. If you don't know what to do and are seeing a woman for the first time, you can say hi or use the Goodbye Introduction. Those moves often lead to opportunities to use your curiosity, either by asking a curiosity question and follow-up questions or by asking "What's the story behind that?"

Other times, you'll find you can go from hi to a Situational Flirting move, making some sort of joke or creative misinterpretation about the environment, and you can bond by being silly and laughing together. Doing that will often lead to good, playful feelings, from which you can also ask a curiosity question or "What's the story behind that?"

Once a woman starts relaxing with you, it's easy to start asking Deepening Questions. You might say, "I know that everyone's job has moments they don't like, but very often there are moments where you feel like, 'Wow, this is what I was put on earth to do.' I'd be curious to know, if you'd care to share, what are some of those moments for you?" From there it's easy to admire what she is into and reflect it back to her, which makes you more special in her eyes and connects you even more.

While this is going on, of course, you've been practicing your Flirting Moves. You've been making and holding eye contact, you've been making decisions quickly and easily, you've been winking at her, you've been complimenting her and so forth. These moves add to the certainty, both on your part and hers, that you are talking to her as a man talks to a woman he is interested in romantically. It will be hard for her to think of you as just a friend; the flirting conversations you've been having also help. At this point you might ask her out for a coffee date. On that date you can do more flirting, more "regular" conversation and Deepening and start asking Romantic Questions.

You can probably sense how all this fits together and how it creates a romantic vibe in your interactions with women. These are the vibes that you can capitalize on to create a sexual relationship. You need never feel stuck in a conversation with a woman again.

AND FINALLY...

Ultimately, the conclusion of this book is written by you. It's written by you in how you live your life and how you use this material. If you look at this as an interesting book that you got a few tips out of, that's fine. But this book will be all the more powerful if you review the program and set it to work. You write the conclusion...in how you use this book in your life.

Even though we don't know you personally, we really do care what happens to you and your success with women. We really do want this book to speak directly to you, and we hope it makes a real and positive difference in your life. We hope to meet you someday at a seminar, through our coaching program or anywhere in the world where we may have the good fortune to connect. We also want to sincerely thank you for reading this book, suspending your doubts and trying things out. We acknowledge you for getting through the sections you might have disagreed with or found difficult. In all sincerity, we commend you for taking the steps you need to take to develop the kind of success with women you desire.

Feel free to contact us and let us know how it goes.

You can reach us:

- via the web at www.howtosucceedwithwomen.com
- via email at Authors@howtosucceedwithwomen.com
- via regular mail at:

Mastery Technologies, Inc.
P.O. Box 55094
Madison, WI 53705

Thanks for Reading This Book

AS A GIFT TO YOU, WE HAVE AN AUDIO SAMPLE OF RON LOUIS AND DAVID COPELAND USING THIS MATERIAL ON WOMEN. YOU CAN DOWNLOAD THIS SAMPLE AT:

www.howtosucceedwithwomen.com/talk

Shy men have a unique and special set of problems. For the last year we have focused our dating coaching practice on working with shy men. Now you can benefit from what we learned in our new audio course, *Overcoming the Nice Guy Syndrome: How to Stop Being Shy Without Becoming a Jerk* (on four audiocassettes or four CDs).

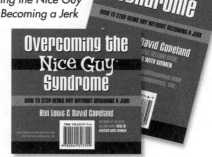

If you are a shy guy, all the "techniques," "pickup lines," or "motivational visualizations" in the world won't help you. The problem deeper than that, and has to be addressed, or you will stay shy. This course addresses those deeper reasons, and gives you concrete, tested ways to become less shy with women.

Imagine going from feeling guilty, afraid, or ashamed with women to feeling good about showing romantic interest, and having it work for both you and the woman! That's what *Overcoming the Nice Guy Syndrome* is about.

These tapes are for you if:

- **You often seem to end up a woman's "friend"** when you would rather be lovers.
- **You have an especially difficult time showing sexual interest** in a woman.
- **Deep down, you feel like showing romantic or sexual interest in a woman is "using" her in some way,** unless you get into a relationship with her.
- **Women feel safe with you, but then go with "bad boys,"** whom you don't want to be like, no matter what the cost.
- **You are especially shy with women** and feel guilty when you try to talk with them.

Imagine...

Being able to both respect women, and let them know about your sexual interest in them...knowing that your intentions with women are good, even if you are only interested in short-term sex...being able to provide both safety and risks for women...not having to control outcomes with women...not being stopped by fear or rejection...being curious about women and life, and letting that guide you.

Imagine being a nice guy who is interesting and exciting to women, and who is able to get sex and relationships with them.

Ordering

Overcoming the Nice Guy Syndrome:
How to Stop Being Shy Without Becoming A Jerk

Overcoming the Nice Guy Syndrome is available on 4 CDs or 4 Cassettes for $59.95 plus $10.00 postage and handling ($40.00 outside of the USA).

Find out more and order online at www.howtosucceedwithwomen.com/tapes/shyguy.html
or use the order form on page 321.

Order form on page 321

THE MASTERY PROGRAM
Your Step-by-Step Course in Meeting, Flirting With, Dating and Seducing the Women of Your Dreams

The Mastery Program Tape Series is 32 professionally-recorded daily lessons on 16 CDs or audiocassettes, including about three hours of tape of us flirting with live women in the studio, along with a 70-page workbook, including special tracking forms. It is designed to teach you every aspect of developing a dating life, from finding "niches" that make it easy to meet women, to knowing what to say when you first approach a woman, to taking a seduction all the way to the bedroom.

Imagine having Ron Louis and David Copeland with you, every day, for over a month, teaching you step-by-step everything you need to know to master the 8 dating "fundamentals" and to have the success with women that you want.

You'll learn:
- How to generate interactions with women that can become romantic
- How to transform your fear of rejection into a friend that powers you toward success
- How to feel really good about your interactions with women, every step of the way
- How and where to meet women, automatically
- How to show your romantic interest in women in ways they will enjoy
- How to overcome your inner "blocks" that stop you with women
- How to flirt with women, ask them out, go for the first kiss, and more!

This course is perfect for any man who feels "stuck" in his dating life with women, and who really wants to jump-start profound improvements in his relationships with women.

Find out more or order online at www.howtosucceedwithwomen.com

or use the order form on page 321.

Order Form On Page 321

There are now more women online than men...and now more than ever, many of these women are attractive and intelligent! But if you don't know where to find these women, or what to say to them via email or using instant message programs, than you'll never have the success you are looking for! This booklet takes you step by step through finding these women, and shows you specifically how to talk with them when you do.

If you are a shy guy, or if you feel nervous around women, the internet is one of the best places for you the flirt with and seduce women—from the comfort of your own home! Learning online flirting skills can be one way for you to increase your confidence with women, and use your shyness as an advantage.

The Internet Seduction Toolkit covers:

- How to use America Online and other Chat clients
- Using "profiles" powerfully
- Secrets of internet personal ads, such as the ones you'll use on popular internet dating sites
- Not making the bonehead mistakes that dating sites seem to try to get you to make
- Touching her heart in the first sentence of your ad
- How to find women online to flirt with, anytime of day or night
- How to create personal "email responders" for handling large numbers of women
- Easy ways to get lots of women into your online flirting "system"
- The five fundamental rules of flirting via email, and how to never break them again
- Real world examples of email interchanges with women that worked, and discussion of the reasons why they worked
- How to turn any Instant Message conversation into a seductive conversation, with numerous real world examples, so you can see exactly how Louis and Copeland are thinking about internet seduction, every step of the way

The Internet Seduction Toolkit costs $11.95 plus $5.95 Postage and Handling in the USA. It is not available to be shipped outside of the USA, except along with orders for our audio courses. If you want to order it from outside the USA, please purchase the electronic, downloadable version at www.howtosucceedwithwomen.com/toolkit/index.html.

Find out more and order online at:
http://www.howtosucceedwithwomen.com/toolkit/index.html
or use the order form on page 321.

Order form

NAME

ADDRESS

SHIPPING ADDRESS (IF DIFFERENT THAN ABOVE)

CREDIT CARD NUMBER

NAME AS IT APPEARS ON THE CARD

EXPIRATION DATE   SIGNATURE

OVERCOMING THE NICE GUY SYNDROME:
HOW TO STOP BEING SHY WITHOUT BECOMING A JERK

☐ 4 CDs   or   ☐ 4 Cassettes for $59.95   _____

THE MASTERY PROGRAM
YOUR STEP-BY-STEP CPOURSE IN MEETING, FLIRTING WITH,
DATING AND SEDUCING THE WOMEN OF YOUR DREAMS

☐ 16 CDs   or   ☐ 16 Cassettes for $247.50   _____

THE INTERNET SEDUCTION TOOLKIT $11.95   _____

SHIPPING AND HANDLING $10.00 ($40.00 outside US)   _____

                                        TOTAL   _____

MAKE CHECKS PAYABLE TO: **MASTERY TECHNOLOGIES, INC.**

MAIL: MASTERY TECHNOLOGIES, INC.
P.O. BOX 55094, MADISON, WI 53705

OR FAX THIS FORM: (608) 663-1550